Living with Nephew

Living with Nephew

How I Got Voted the Meanest Parent in the World

SHERRI L. BURR

RMK PUBLISHING

Albuquerque, New Mexico

Living with Nephew: How I Got Voted the Meanest Parent in the World

Hardback ISBN: 979-8-9904249-8-2
Paperback ISBN: 9798275109665
Published by RMK Publications
Published in the United States

PRAISE FOR
Living with Nephew

"Oh, what a charmer Sherri Burr's book is. Can you imagine what happens when the twelve-year-old nephew comes to spend a year with his single Auntie? They both find terror and wisdom—so will the reader. Buy it now. Read it now. Laugh and learn forever."

Max Evans, Author

The Hi-Lo Country, The Rounders, Madam Millie, and *Faraway Blue*

"Wow – a tremendous story. I really liked how the author weaves in stories of her love life. This book is hilarious yet has a bittersweet ending that brought tears to my eyes."

Melody Groves, Author

Before Billy the Kid: The Boy Behind the Legendary Outlaw

"I was a witness to a devoted auntie's dedication to her Nephew and his antics. Sherri's fun stories demonstrate the love and affection both auntie and Nephew have for each other."

Kathleen A. Hessler, J.D., R.N., Author

Promise Me, Daughter, A Nurse Attorney Navigates Her Mother's Early-Onset Alzheimer's

“Sherri Burr's account of parenting her 12-year-old nephew in his seventh-grade year is by turns hilarious and poignant. There is a lot of wisdom in these pages about life, learning and love. The honesty of both Auntie and Nephew makes this a riveting tale.”

Dr. Suzanne Geissler Bowles, Author
God and Sea Power

“This book has wonderful energy. When law professor Sherri Burr invites twelve-year-old Nephew to live with her, she transforms both her world and his. *Living with Nephew* leads the reader on a hilarious and weighty adventure. Sherri and Nephew challenge and educate each other. And in the process, each becomes a better person. You will love this memoir.”

Judith S. Avila, NYT bestselling Author
Code Talker: The first and only memoir by one of the original Navajo code talkers of WWII.

“Charming is the right word. I could see this selling to all mothers in “recovery.”

Dr. Sue Brown
Retired Pediatrician, UNM School of Medicine

"Sherri Burr is a talented storyteller, and her book is incredibly moving. In *Living with Nephew*, Sherri captures the complexities of devastating family events, including domestic violence, abandonment, and sexual abuse, in a way that showcases resilience and strength instead of bitterness and defeat."

Theresa Mancuso, Occupational Therapist

DEDICATION

For my great-grandmother Zellar, grandmother Ola Belle, great-aunt Callie, mother Ola Mae, and Aunt Liz who paved the path of family caregiving that I would later walk. May you rest in peace.

AUTHOR'S NOTE

This is a work of creative nonfiction. I portray these events based on my recollections. While all the stories in this book are true, some of the names and identifying details have been changed to protect the privacy of those involved. The first time I use a fictionalized name, I place it in "quotes."

I started writing this book in 2005 to chronicle the experience of parenting my nephew. In 2006, an early draft of the manuscript won second place in the SouthWest Writers Annual Contest for Nonfiction Books.

An early draft of the manuscript also received praise from authors Max Evans, Tony Hillerman, and Wally "Famous" Amos. Even though these men have since died, their blubs appear on the back cover and in the book along with those of other authors. I am grateful to them for the letters and emails they sent confirming permission to use their words of praise in this book.

Several family members are mentioned in this book. For easy reference, here's a chart showing their separate relationships to me and Nephew.

FAMILY MEMBERS

Name of Family Member	*Relationship to Sherri*	*Relationship to Nephew*
Mance Easter	Great-grandfather	Great-great-grandfather
Rev. & Mrs. Smead P. Easter	Grandpa and Granny	Great-grandparents
Ola Mae Burr Peete	Mother	Grandmother/Granny
John Lincoln Burr	Father	
Alex Peete	Stepfather	Grandfather
Ralph and Terrance, Butch, Vera	Sibling and Half-Siblings	Uncles and Aunt
Ida, Liz, Gussie, and Bubba, John, Charles	Aunts and Uncles	Great Aunts and Great Uncles

Sherri L. Burr

TABLE OF CONTENTS

Chapter 1 I'm So Cute! 1

Chapter 2 She Wants to Marry Me and Have My Kids 19

Chapter 3 I'm Going to Stay a Virgin Until I Get Married 27

Chapter 4 I Just Mopped that Floor 33

Chapter 5 Hypothetically Speaking 43

Chapter 6 She Wants to Fourth-Base Me 47

Chapter 7 Why Can't You Just Whip Me Like a Normal Parent 51

Chapter 8 He Thinks You're Feeding Me Rabbit Food 63

Chapter 9 I Got in a Fight at School Today 77

Chapter 10 I Dreamed I Jumped Off the Balcony 85

Chapter 11 I'm Going to Give a Paaaarty 93

Chapter 12 She Wants to Give Me All of Her 107

Chapter 13 You Just Act Mean 113

Chapter 14 I was On TV Last Night 119

Chapter 15 Two Weeks 129

Chapter 16 I Would have Dumped Her on the Spot 145

Chapter 18 Don't Scream 159

Chapter 19 Those Vultures will Swarm 171

Chapter 20 Yes, Auntie, I Did It 179

Chapter 21 What are You Doing Going Through My Trash 185

Chapter 21 Can I Come Back 195

Chapter 23 That Doctor's a Total Loser 209

Chapter 24 I Didn't Think She was Ovulating 213

Chapter 25 You're Sending Me Back to Joblessness and Homelessness 217

Chapter 26 She Didn't Know 227
Chapter 27 I Can Catch the Next Plane 231
Chapter 28 How Information Becomes Transformation 247
Chapter 29 Here's the Phone 257
Acknowledgements 265
Other Books by Sherri Burr 267
About the Author 269

Chapter 1

I'M SO CUTE!

My nephew Terrance moonwalked into my heart when he was eleven-months old. I had sent my half-sister Vera a round-trip ticket to fly from Long Beach, California, to bring our brother's first child to our grandmother's seventy-eighth birthday party in Phoenix. Vera walked in while carrying Terrance and sat him down. He immediately walked backward, Michael Jackson style. Mom, Granny, and I applauded.

Phoenix seemed like a natural location for us to meet my first nephew and Mom's first grandchild. Granny and Grandpa's three-bedroom ranch house had large front and back yards containing Granny's carefully tended vegetable garden along with her grapefruit, orange, lemon, and peach trees. A grapevine snaked up a trellis near the carport. We congregated in the backyard with South Mountain's peaks and valleys in view.

In the mid-1950s, Grandpa and Granny had joined The Great Migration, the movement of six million African Americans out of the rural Southern United States to the Northeast, Midwest, and West. Grandpa, who suffered from asthma, had asked his church to transfer him to drier climates, and it rotated him throughout the Southwest, including Arizona, California, New Mexico, and Texas.

Even after settling in Arizona, they made frequent return trips to Arkansas. When I was one-month old, Granny took me by train to visit relatives in Hope, where she had been born. The town would later become famous for having been the birthplace of President Bill Clinton. His grandfather's store was located within walking distance of their home, which my grandparents kept for quite a while before selling it.

My father John's family had migrated from Oklahoma to Phoenix in the 1950s. Indeed, his family had begun their American sojourn in Virginia where his fourth great-grandparents and their toddler son, Gideon Hill, had been freed from slavery in 1787. Gideon's grandson (my second great-grandfather) had served in the Civil War before moving from Virginia to Ohio, where he worked for a congressman. This second great-grandfather later relocated to Texas, where my great-grandmother Zellar was born. She moved on to Oklahoma where she married and gave birth to John's mother, Juanita, as her last child. When she came of age, Juanita moved to Phoenix where she purchased a home and set up a beauty salon.

After Mom married John, Aunt Liz spoke of his family with reverence. John, however, failed to impress

Granny who thought him too attractive with his "gamine-shaped eyes" to be a serious person.

During my childhood, Granny and Grandpa frequently opened their home to their children, grandchildren, and other relatives when their homes disappeared for one reason or another. My mother and her kids became recipients of their generosity.

Just after I turned nineteen months old, my good-looking father John left pregnant Mom and me to find his fame and fortune gambling in Las Vegas. Our electricity had been turned off and there was little food in the refrigerator. Neighbors alerted Grandpa to our plight, and he rescued us. We moved in with Granny and Grandpa until after Mom gave birth to Ralph.

Realizing she was on her own, Mom went to nursing school so she could take care of us with little support from John, despite his coming from a family that was far wealthier than Mom's. Between her studies and working, Mom taught me to read before I turned three.

When I was six and Ralph four, Mom became involved with light-skinned Alexander Peete from Morenci, Arizona, where he had grown up speaking fluent Spanish. He drove a delivery truck for the Coca-Cola Bottling Company. On the surface, this seemed a better match than the one with my father, John, since Alex was gainfully employed. Poor Mom, however, went from divorcing a professional gambler from a respected family to marrying an alcoholic. With Alex, she had four children (Terrance, Butch, Vera, and Tony Jeffrey) in rapid succession.

As an adult, Terrance was the first to have children. He named his son a junior after himself. Immediately following the first meeting at Granny's house, I started calling my new nephew "the Kid" to distinguish him from his father.

Mom objected, saying, "A kid is a goat." She proclaimed him "T Junior," and I settled on "Nephew." That felt right.

About six months after first meeting Nephew, I sent his mother Mary a ticket to come visit me in New Mexico. I had moved to Albuquerque two years before Nephew was born to start teaching at the University of New Mexico School of Law.

My first Albuquerque apartment was a two-story, three-bedroom penthouse designed by celebrated award-winning architect, Antoine Predock. Architectural students flocked from all over the world to photograph the soft blue, purple, and pink building. I wanted to tell them that while the complex was beautiful on the outside, it suffered from problematic construction.

Whenever it rained, the penthouse roof leaked. I placed buckets throughout the upstairs kitchen to capture enough water to care for my plants. After several rains during New Mexico's monsoon season, the entire drywall peeled off in the upstairs bathroom. Water even managed to travel downstairs from the top floor through the walls to the master bedroom on the lower floor. Bed placement became problematic when water dripped from the light fixture in the ceiling. I finally gave up trying to manage the leaks and moved to a sturdier two-bedroom, two-bathroom adobe townhouse in Albuquerque's North Valley.

After I picked up Mary and Nephew from the airport and brought them to my new rental, she seemed disappointed to see the one-story structure because my brother Butch had described a gorgeous penthouse apartment from his visit. I explained to Mary that Butch had traveled to Albuquerque during the dry season.

Knowing my excitement about my nephew's visit, my colleague "Carmen" invited us to her home for a breakfast of pancakes and strawberries. Carmen introduced Nephew to her three-and-a-half-year-old daughter, "Florella," who joined us for the meal. When eighteen-month-old Nephew announced, "I've got to go pee," Carmen was astonished. "It freaks me out to see a kid that young talking and already potty-trained," she said.

A couple of months later during a break from teaching, I flew to Los Angeles to pick-up Nephew and bring him back to Albuquerque. Mary had dressed him in an attractive blue jean outfit before handing him over at the gate. At the door of the airplane, I put him down and he walked through the Southwest Airlines plane like a conquering knight returning to his people. As a sea of heads turned to look at twenty-month-old Nephew, I thought *My, this kid has presence.*

At our seats toward the back of the plane in the days before family boarding, Nephew immediately began talking to all the nearby ladies. He said, "Hi. What's your name? My name is Terrance." And so it went until he found one whose name was Sherry. He turned to me and said, "Her name is Sherry and your name is Sherri."

Nephew charmed women he met on planes and elsewhere. He was rewarded by their comments on how cute he was. In that sense, he was like his father. I remembered when Mom took my brother Terrance to grocery stores, women rushed over and talk about what a cute baby he was. By the time Nephew was three, he had heard the word "cute" referred to him so often that I caught him one day staring in the mirror, pinching his cheeks, and declaring to himself, "I'm so cute."

When he noticed me looking at him in horror, he turned and said, "You're cute, too, Auntie Sherri."

I burst into laughter.

That afternoon, we went to a Hastings superstore to rent two videos. I told him he could pick one and I would pick the other. He chose *The Lion King*. As we were standing in line to check out, Nephew picked up a giant candy bar and said, "Buy me this."

"No," I said. "Put that down."

"You're mean, Auntie Sherri."

"If I'm mean, put this video back," I replied, handing him *The Lion King*.

"Then you'd be doubly mean," another customer piped in.

That was just one of many occasions when people eavesdropped on our conversations and added their few cents. It happened so often I began to wonder if it was unusual for parent figures to talk to kids.

St. Francis Child Care Center often took care of Nephew when I had to teach at the University of New Mexico Law School. One day I picked him up and noticed he was rubbing his cheeks.

"What's wrong?" I asked.

He pointed to a little girl and said horrified, "She kissed me."

The girl's mother who worked at St. Francis explained that the minute I dropped off my then four-year-old nephew, her three-year-old daughter had grabbed him. She kissed him again after he performed an Elvis impersonation.

"Elvis?" I asked, surprised.

"Yeah. We had a singer playing Elvis's music and Terrance really liked him," the mother said.

That evening, we went to the grocery store. As I walked down the produce aisle, I noticed Nephew gyrating his hips and singing, "You ain't nothing but a hound dog/Cryin' all the time." People gathered around. I grabbed Nephew and laughingly apologized to the onlookers.

Each passing year seemed to magnify Nephew's self-confidence. After he turned five, he began flying nonstop from Los Angeles to Albuquerque by himself. He liked life in New Mexico so much he asked if he could live with me for a year and attend school. Since he was already visiting for about two months a year, I thought, *Why not nine months?* After all, both sides of my family had a history of taking in family members for long stretches of time. My paternal great-grandmother Zellar had raised my father, John, for seven years before his mother sent for him to join her in Phoenix. *If other family members had previously helped raised the next generation, so could I, right?*

When Nephew started first grade in California, he was placed on a year-round schedule that left him with odd three-week breaks. This made arranging childcare difficult for his mother Mary, who had separated from my brother Terrance and become a school bus driver. To help her out, I flew Nephew to Albuquerque. Indeed, I sent so many plane tickets that Mary reported that the minute one arrived in the mail, Nephew went into his room and packed his bag. While he visited me, I tried to give him options and teach him responsibilities.

Once while playing outside my rental condo located in the foothills of Albuquerque's Sandia Mountains, Nephew rang the doorbell, opened the front door, and yelled in his loudest voice, "Auntie Sherri."

When I came to look at him from the upper floor landing, Nephew said, "I stepped in dog poop!"

"You stay right there," I said. "Don't come inside. I'll be right down." I gathered a pail of soapy water and a scrub brush before descending the stairs. "Here," I said, handing six-year-old Nephew the items. "Use this to clean the dog poop off the sidewalk and your shoes."

"Okay, Auntie," he said.

It took him two hours to clean up, partly because he frequently stopped to talk with neighbors who asked what he was doing. Some of them thought I was being too harsh not to help him, but I told them I wasn't the one who stepped in dog poop. To this day, he has never made that mistake again, although he often showed chutzpah in other circumstances.

During the visit, six-year-old Nephew and one of his friends accompanied me to the opening celebration of the Montaño Bridge. As a specialist in Art Law, I had been appointed by the mayor to the Albuquerque's Arts Board, which selects art to adorn capital improvement projects. After the event, we trekked back to my car and ran into Mayor Martin Chavez. I introduced the boys. Nephew asked him for a ride to our car because he and his friend were tired. Mayor Chavez willingly agreed, and we all piled into his SUV. For Nephew, the mayor's title had little significance. What counted was that the mayor's car was closer than ours, and he could hitch a ride.

* * *

One October, I picked him up from St. Francis Child Care Center to take him to the airport for his return trip to California. He asked me to wait a minute. He returned carrying a twenty-pound pumpkin. "I picked it myself on our fieldtrip," he declared with pride.

"They'll never let you take it on the plane," I said, astonished, as the pumpkin weighed about half as much as he did.

"Yes, they will," he assured me.

At the airport, we placed the pumpkin on the conveyer belt, and it passed security screening. After we boarded the Southwest Airlines flight, a kind gentleman placed the pumpkin in the overhead space. When the plane landed, the gentleman offered to carry the pumpkin to the door and give it to Nephew right before we exited. Nephew took the pumpkin and triumphantly walked out to meet his mother. The people in line to catch the next Southwest Airlines flight clapped as they saw a seven-year-old boy carrying a gigantic pumpkin.

***

Later that year I moved to Honolulu to begin a stint teaching law at the University of Hawaii. A UH professor asked me to exchange posts so he could be nearer to his doctor girlfriend who had been transferred to El Paso, Texas. I bought an old blue Volvo and rented a two-bedroom, two-bathroom townhouse with its own boat dock. Since my new rental townhome was situated just a few paddles away from the Pacific Ocean, I purchased a lime green kayak from a UH colleague. I loved using it after a long teaching day. It seemed when I stroked into the ocean, all stresses drifted away with the tide.

I called seven-year-old Nephew to ask how he felt about flying to Hawaii to see me during his spring break from second grade. I told him that while the flight to Albuquerque was only two hours, the flight to

Honolulu takes five to six hours. He said he could handle it.

As I waited at the Honolulu gate for his plane to arrive, I cried softly. I felt blessed to continue my relationship with my half-brother's son even though I had moved to a different state.

Nephew's plane landed, and several strangers walked up and said, "You must be Terrance's Auntie Sherri."

When Nephew finally deplaned, I asked him, "Did you speak to everyone on the plane?"

He replied, "I was bored so I helped the flight attendants pass out mints. When people asked where I was going, I told them I'd be visiting my Auntie Sherri in Honolulu."

As we walked toward baggage claim, more strangers greeted him.

"Hi, Terrance."

"Have fun, Terrance."

"Enjoy Hawaii, Terrance."

Although Nephew had just arrived, he seemed to know more people in Honolulu than I did. I told him that we had to go to the University of Hawaii law school before I could take him to my place. "You're going to meet Supreme Court Justice Ruth Bader Ginsburg," I said.

"Who's that?" he asked.

"She's a judge on our country's highest court," I explained. "Also, there will be lots of Hawaiian food and dancing."

"Now, that's cool."

After the law school ceremony, we lined up at the reception to be introduced to the shy Justice, who would later become an icon referred to as "The Notorious RBG." When others posed for pictures with her, they hesitated to put their arms around her. When it was our turn to meet Justice Ginsburg, she placed her hand on Nephew's shoulders. She somehow felt comfortable around this outgoing child.

When we arrived at my rental townhouse, Nephew announced, "I have a girlfriend."

Startled, I asked, "Is she in your second-grade class?"

"Oh, No," he said, emphatically. "I like older women. She's in fifth grade."

I smiled, relieved that he had not yet gone through puberty.

The next day, my Navy lieutenant friend Sean and I took Nephew out in the Pacific Ocean in my lime green kayak. I had met the six-foot, three-inch Sean through the Soul Food Sunday's group of mostly military folks who took turns hosting a rotating dinner. One of our dinners at my townhome featured Hawaii's then Lieutenant Governor (later U.S. Senator) Mazie Hirono.

Sean, Nephew and I capsized as waves hit the kayak sideways on our trip into the Pacific. Sean rescued Nephew as I yelled, "Save Terrance. The family will never forgive me if something happens to him." Like me, Nephew had been born first in his generation and the family was particularly protective of him.

As it turned out, we were in two feet of water so my panic and the fear on Nephew's face were for naught.

A few days later, we attended a Hawaiian second-grade class so Nephew could compare what it was like to go to school in a different state. We discussed whether Nephew should spend the next year going to school in Honolulu. I concluded that it would be too difficult. I had to drive away from my rental townhouse at 6:30 a.m. to beat the rush hour traffic heading from the Hawaii Kai area to arrive in time to teach in Manoa at 8:00 a.m. I couldn't begin to contemplate how I could also get Nephew to school within that time window. Also, I didn't yet have a deep stock of friends to help, like in New Mexico. So, we dismissed the idea.

That December, Nephew as an eight-year-old flew to Hawaii again. By then I had met Wally "Famous" Amos when one of my students invited him to speak to our Intellectual Property class. Wally was such an inspirational speaker that I asked him to be my first guest on my new cable access television show called "Arts Talk." Wally agreed. After the taping, Wally invited me to come over to his home during the holiday season. I brought Nephew with me, and we spent the evening chatting while baking a batch of chocolate chip cookies with Famous Amos. As we left, Wally autographed one of his children's books for Nephew.

My nearly twenty months visiting in Hawaii eventually came to an end and I returned to my position at the University of New Mexico. I loved the Hawaiian people and culture, and fought back tears as I boarded the plane. My exchange partner had resigned from his UH professorship, and I was asked by administrators to apply for his position. After I was informed that I would have to give up tenure and start all over again with none of my prior scholarship to be considered, my head won out over my heart. I returned to Albuquerque to teach.

* * *

Nephew continued to visit me during his school breaks. On one of these trips, a man exited the Southwest Airlines flight and walked right over to me. He introduced himself, handed me his business card, and said, "I invited Terrance to come horseback riding at my ranch." The situation reminded me of waiting for Terrance to deplane in Honolulu.

After the flight attendants brought out Nephew and I signed their paperwork, I asked him about the gentleman. "He was so nice and interesting, Auntie. He has a lot of horses. Can we please go riding? Please!" Nephew said.

I obliged Nephew's request and set up a horseback riding expedition. Nephew was mounted on a gentle Paint named Freckles. After I explained that I could ride Western, Eastern, and Bareback with no reigns, I was given a more robust horse. It was fun riding trails with Nephew and our guide. I later found a toy horse that looked like Freckles and gave him to Nephew as a memento.

When he turned 10, Nephew flew to Little Rock, Arkansas to join Mom, Ralph, and me on a family trip. I had started my Arkansas sojourn a few days early to attend a conference at the University of Arkansas, Fayetteville. I spoke on a panel while former Surgeon General Jocelyn Elders keynoted the event. We chatted for a while and I explained my mother, who had grown up in Hope, was on her way for a visit. Dr. Elders invited my family to visit her for lunch. I would have been happy with sandwiches and was amazed that Dr. Elders cooked a feast for us with vegetables from her own garden, fish caught by her husband, and other delicious treats. Since her husband and Mom had gone to rival Arkansas high schools, they discussed old games and championships.

After our visit with Dr. Elders, we headed in two cars down to Hope with Ralph driving Nephew and me driving Mom. We found President Bill Clinton's childhood home about a mile from Mom's childhood home, and his relatives buried in the same cemetery as hers. We found a headstone for her grandfather Mance Easter, a minister and undertaker, whom Mom remembered with reverence and fondness. Fascinated that a chain-link fence separated white and black sections, I later wrote "Segregation still not laid to rest in Hope cemetery" as one of my Thursday *Albuquerque Tribune*'s columns.

Nephew brought with him a straight-A report card to Arkansas. During the prior Christmas vacation, I had promised him a computer if he produced straight A's before he graduated from middle school. I was astonished to have to pay up during his fifth-grade year.

Eventually, I agreed Nephew could live with me during his seventh-grade year. In June 2001, I purchased a two-story, four-bedroom, three-bathroom townhouse near the university. Nephew was visiting when I moved in, and he met my neighbor Mildred after she knocked on the door to greet us. Mildred handed me a telephone list for everyone in our townhome community and asked for my telephone numbers. In her mid-seventies, Mildred sported a full head of whitish-silver hair, a sincere countenance, and seemed so welcoming that I immediately gave her both my landline and university telephone numbers.

For the fall and spring semesters of 2002-2003, the University of New Mexico had approved a sabbatical leave from my job to write a book. I thought I could easily include a stint at single parenting.

The numerous visits throughout the years turned out to be little preparation for Nephew moving in. I should have been forewarned that this would not be easy. His mother had placed him on punishment up until the day he left for New Mexico because he had lied to her and thrown away his sixth-grade report card containing three F's. Nephew, himself, had changed his mind about wanting to spend a year with me after realizing he would miss his friends. His mother, however, insisted he move to Albuquerque. Mary was so emphatic that I became alarmed by her eagerness to get rid of him.

After talking to Nephew, we agreed he should fly out in late July to attend the inaugural Georgia O'Keeffe Art and Leadership Camp for Boys and return to start seventh grade in Long Beach. Closer to his departure date, however, he called and asked if he could stay in Albuquerque until December.

"Fine," I said. "You're welcome to stay as long as you like." Nephew had moonwalked into my heart when he was eleven months old, and now he was moving into my home. I thought that at age twelve, Nephew would no longer need babysitters when I attended evening events and would not have seriously discovered girls. My prediction was only half right.

Chapter 2

SHE WANTS TO MARRY ME AND HAVE MY KIDS

I need to call "Kiana" to see how she's taking this separation," Nephew said after arriving in my home at the beginning of August 2002 to spend the year attending seventh grade in New Mexico. By age twelve, he had grown to four-foot, eleven-inches tall with over 130 pounds of liberal fat attached to his frame. He possessed skin the color of a Hershey's chocolate bar and fleshy cheeks, the kind adults loved to pinch on young kids. Long eyelashes shielded his luminous, almond-shaped eyes.

"Of course, you can use the phone, Nephew. I can get you a calling card for your long-distance calls. Will that be okay?" I asked.

"Sure Auntie. While I'm here, my Mother wants me to bring up my grades. She's upset about my F's."

"I can see why. How does someone go from straight A's in fifth grade to three F's in the sixth? That takes some doing."

"Not if you don't turn in your work," he said, emphatically.

"Hopefully, we can change that while you're here. Go call Kiana."

That week, I drove two hours round-trip every day to Santa Fe in my un-air-conditioned maroon-colored Daihatsu Rocky, which looked like a small Jeep, to take Nephew to the Georgia O'Keeffe Art and Leadership Camp for Boys. Despite the striking mountain scenery on I-25, traveling in the one-hundred-degree New Mexico heat drained me. As I waited for Nephew during the day, I used the time to look for an air-conditioned car. I found several Saabs and had them checked out by Smart Motors. After the mechanic told me one needed only a few repairs, I bought a six-year-old silver Saab and rejoiced in the cool air.

Nephew seemed to benefit from the O'Keeffe camp, as it taught him appreciation for his poetry and song-writing abilities. He also learned yoga and went on overnight camping trips. That day in the newly purchased air-conditioned Saab, he sang one of his original songs for me as we drove back to Albuquerque. I clapped when he finished belting out his tune in a soulful, melodic voice. *Nephew has some talent.*

Several days after arriving in Albuquerque, Nephew decided to break up with Kiana. "I'm too young to be in such a serious relationship," he said. "She wants to marry me and have my kids. We're only twelve. Besides, I'm going to meet more girls here." After discussing the situation with his best friend in California, Nephew announced over dinner his best friend would tell Kiana's best friend to tell Kiana he was ending their relationship.

"Yikes," I said. "That's a coward's way out."

"What can I do?" he asked, with his hands raised in frustration. "She won't let me go."

"But she's in Long Beach. It's not like she's going to show up on our doorstep in Albuquerque."

He shrugged.

* * *

Nine days later, Kiana belonged to the dustbins of his relationship history. By the tenth day, Nephew had another girlfriend, Florella, the five-foot, five-inch Hispanic daughter of my friend Carmen. He referred to her as "What's her name."

When I gave him an astonished look, he added, "Well, she doesn't know my name either."

"Okay," I said. "It sounds like the beginning of a beautiful friendship, as they say in the movies."

New to single parenthood, I inadvertently facilitated this romance. I took them to see *Lord of the Rings*, thinking they were just friends, and dropped them off. They had first met when he was one and she was three over a breakfast of pancakes and strawberries. As I drove up to collect Nephew and Florella from the movies, the now twelve- and fourteen-year-old youths were sitting side-by-side with no space in between, playing a video game on my cell phone. They climbed into the back seat of the Silver Saab. On the way to Florella's house, I glanced in the rear-view mirror and noticed they were holding hands.

After arriving at her house, Nephew walked Florella to her front door.

"What's going on?" I asked when he climbed into the backseat.

"I got with her during the movie," he said.

"You did what?" I exclaimed.

"During the movies I kissed her and said, 'I guess this means you're my girlfriend.' She said, 'You haven't asked me yet.' I asked her, and she said, 'Yes'."

This coupling brought ten calls a day. "Is Terrance there?" were the first words I heard after picking up the phone. To call him for dinner, I no longer had to shout up to his bedroom on the second floor of my townhome. Since he was constantly on the phone, I just hit the speaker-phone button and said, "Terrance, dinner's ready."

It soon occurred to me that Kiana in California was the ideal girlfriend from my perspective. She had never called.

I told Carmen, Florella's mother, that I expected her daughter to dump Terrance once school started. "After all," I said, "is Florella going to want her high school friends to know she has a seventh-grade boyfriend?"

"I don't know," Carmen responded. "She likes him. He's awfully cute."

Nephew overheard our conversation and protested my pessimism. "Auntie, it's going to last."

"Fine," I said. "I bet you a dollar it won't last until August thirty-first."

Two days before school began, I registered Nephew at Jefferson Middle School. With its beautiful buildings topped with red tile roofs, Jefferson had been established in 1939, the year of my mother's birth. The school was a little over a mile from my home. My colleague who specialized in family law suggested having Nephew's parents write an agreement giving me custody over him for the academic year. Since my brother Terrance and Mary were no longer together, I had them sign the agreement separately. Jefferson accepted the paperwork.

I was surprised to read the registration card's listing of Nephew's race as White/Caucasian. I pointed out the mistake to Mrs. Schroeder, Nephew's science teacher, who was accepting the cards. She told me to just correct the form. I crossed out White/Caucasian and wrote Black/African American. When I pre-registered Nephew in May, the Caucasian counselor met both of us. My skin is the color of a Godiva Chocolate Truffle and nearly as dark as Nephew's. We obviously presented as African Americans.

Before moving to New Mexico, I had heard that within New Mexico's traditional tri-cultural communities of Anglos, Hispanics, and Indians, Blacks were considered honorary Anglos. New Mexico has a proud heritage and unique approach to race. Taos Pueblo in the north is one of the oldest continuously occupied establishments in the world. The Spanish conquistadors encountered the Indians in the 1500s when Albuquerque and Santa Fe were settled. The Anglos came later. This was the first evidence I'd seen of Blacks being lumped in with the Anglos. That didn't happen when my mother was growing up in segregated Hope, Arkansas.

Nephew began seventh grade at Jefferson Middle School on August fifteenth. The first day, I walked him down the street to take the bus. I found myself crying as I walked home. It was hard to believe that my moonwalking 11-month-old nephew was now twelve years old and in the seventh grade.

* * *

I remembered how excited I had been to begin my seventh-grade year at Lassen Junior High School in Phoenix. It was the first time I had different teachers for different subjects. Life inside our home, however, was a lot less fun. Mom's second husband Alex often came home drunk the day he got his paycheck. One time he brought a side of beef with him. Mom had to give away over half of it because we didn't have room in our refrigerator's freezer to store that many pounds of meat.

Another time after receiving his paycheck, Alex brought home a rabbit, which became my two-year old sister Vera's pet, the first for her. At age twelve I had my collie Princess, ten-year-old Ralph his German shepherd King, five-year-old Terrance his cat Coco and he shared black-as-midnight poodles named Amos and Andy with four-year-old Butch.

Then there were the times when Alex stumbled home consumed by rage. He expressed his anger by either hitting Mom or slamming her head up against walls or car doors. This made Ralph and me livid, but as I was barely over five-foot and Ralph was still a lot less than five foot, we felt helpless to counter our stepfather's drunken actions.

I hoped this seventh-grade year would be a lot better for Nephew.

Chapter 3

I'M GOING TO STAY A VIRGIN UNTIL I GET MARRIED

Nephew was thrilled to be attending Jefferson. As the new kid from California, he became an instant celebrity. The second day of school, a classmate asked him to be her boyfriend. "I told her I was already taken," he announced proudly over a chicken and rice dinner that evening.

"That's wonderful that you're being faithful to Florella," I replied. "I might end up owing you a dollar after all."

As our conversation continued, Nephew told me that he wasn't qualified to take the bus because he lived within two miles of school. The next morning, I walked slightly over a mile with him to Jefferson, pointing out places where my friends lived in case he ever encountered an emergency.

Four days later, Nephew walked in the door and handed me a dollar. A different girl had asked him to be her boyfriend. He explained he discovered caramel-colored "Michelle" and asked *her* to be his girlfriend. Now he had a problem. How was he going to get rid of Florella since he didn't know her best friend? He wanted to just stop calling her and hope she'd take a hint.

That week as he was deciding how to give Florella the news, Michelle dumped *him*. Their budding relationship had lasted a day and a half. "What happened?" I asked, as we munched on a dinner salad.

"She thought I was telling everyone that we were going out. She handed me a note that said, 'You told everyone we were going out. Now tell everyone we're not.'"

"Oh. Aren't you glad you still have Florella?" I asked.

"No, because I'm talking to 'Beverly'."

* * *

The next evening, we discussed the Florella situation with my friend Jamie who suggested Nephew call Florella to ask if they could remain friends. He did. She agreed.

Nephew then created a triangle as he called Beverly while continuing to woo back Michelle. Neither classmate wanted to be his girlfriend. The five-foot, six-inch Beverly said he was too short.

A week later, he announced that during passing period he acquired a new girlfriend, "Seisha." "My friends are teasing me," he said. "They want to know how I could go out with someone with such a big nose."

Seisha called twice that evening.

Forty-seven hours after it began, Seisha was no more. "What happened?" I asked in what has become routine dinner conversation.

"I heard she was going to dump me to go back to her former boyfriend, so I sent her friend to tell her it was over."

"What did she say?"

"She said she was about to dump me. That's the difference between black and Hispanic girls. Black girls always say, 'I was just about to dump him.' Hispanic girls never say that."

Whoa, I thought, at twelve was he becoming an expert on inter-racial dating? There was one thing I did not want him to become an expert on, at least not under my watch, and that was sex. When I asked him what he did with his girlfriends, he said, "Oh, we kiss and hold hands. I made my mother a promise that I'm going to stay a virgin until I get married."

My lawyer skills kicked in, and I wanted a modified version of his pledge in writing. I asked him to sign a contract to remain a virgin during his year in New Mexico.

He agreed, but was reluctant to accept the provision that, if his grades drop below a 3.0 or a B average, he must forfeit his female privileges (no calls, no girlfriends). He argued that wasn't fair.

I pointed out that obtaining better grades was his priority. He finally signed the contract after I agreed to use my frequent flier miles to send him to France if he obtained a 4.0 average on any one report card. He was studying French, and his class was fundraising to travel to Paris the next summer.

* * *

Nephew walked in the door from school one day with a look of amazement. "Auntie," he said, "Did you know one of your neighbors pushes a baby buggy with a cat inside?"

"That's "Olga." She's from Germany," I said, as if that explained her behavior.

"Don't you think that's weird?" Nephew responded.

"Yeah, but what do you want me to do? Rescue the cat?"

"No. It's just weird."

"Welcome to life in New Mexico. Besides, that cat could hop out anytime it wants."

"Have you seen your other neighbor walking in the morning?" Nephew asked.

"Which one?" I questioned.

"The one in her white bathrobe. She walks around the block while drinking coffee and being followed by a dog with one of those lampshade collars."

"Oh, that's "Trudy." She's from Australia, and her hound is deaf and blind. I think she uses the collar to shield the dog from the sun."

"What kind of neighborhood is this?" he asked, shaking his head.

"You're not in Long Beach anymore," I said.

"That's the truth. These people wouldn't last five minutes in the 'hood."

"Neither would you. One of these days, we should go to New York City or Chicago so you can see what a real ghetto looks like."

"That's okay. We got enough brothers killing each other in L.A.," he said, as if he was a seasoned observer of society's social ills.

"At least my neighbors are harmless," I said.

"Yeah, and weird," he said, getting in the last word.

* * *

When I was in seventh grade, my family lived in a neighborhood situated at the base of Phoenix's South Mountain. Our neighbors weren't weird, and outside of our home my brothers and I found bliss in the constant sunshine. I led my brothers Ralph, Terrance and Butch on jackrabbit hunting expeditions in the mountains. We would trek along counting the creatures as they scurried away.

When we weren't hiking, Ralph and I popped wheelies on our bikes or would knock on neighborhood doors until we found kids to play with. Fortunately, our Mexican American neighbors down the street had ten children. We thought they were lucky to have enough kids to form two basketball teams. For me, boys were playmates rather than objects of affection.

I particularly liked playing football with Ralph and his friends because it was a game of strategy. My favorite positions were quarterback and running back. I had a slight advantage because I ran fast, and the boys wouldn't tackle me if they couldn't pull the flag out of my back pocket. However, I didn't feel prohibited from attacking them. If it helped to keep one from scoring a touchdown, I leapt into the air, landed on the boy, brought him to the ground, and then removed his flag.

Mom didn't like me playing football because she said it wasn't a lady-like activity. She bought lots of Barbie's, but I became bored with them after I cut their hair. When Mom refused to buy me jeans to play football, I borrowed a pair of Ralph's cutoffs. He complained that I stretched them out because I was slightly bigger than him. However, when he needed another person for his football team, he accepted that I had to wear his play clothes.

Outside of attending church on Sundays, that's how us kids spent our weekends and afternoons. I regularly taught Sunday School to a variety of ages from preschoolers to grade schoolers and played the piano for various services. Come Monday morning, we would be back on the bus headed for school

.

Chapter 4

I JUST MOPPED THAT FLOOR

Nephew had been attending Jefferson Middle School for about a month when he said to me out of the blue, "You look like you need a vacation."

Yeah from you, I thought. Instead, I said, "Thanks for letting me know I look tired."

The reality was that I felt worn out. The extra responsibilities of shopping, cleaning house, and cooking for Nephew were taking a toll. I began to question whether I was cut out for single parenthood. While reading the morning newspaper, I saw that John Rosemond, a syndicated columnist who writes on parenting, was coming to New Mexico to give two seminars in one day. I signed up for both, desperate for advice.

On a Saturday in late September, I sat in the audience as Rosemond told us what has gone wrong with parenting in America. He advised putting the care of ourselves and our marriages before our children.

I could tell the audience didn't like it when Rosemond said that putting children first in the family made them "manipulative, demanding, and unappreciative" of things that parents do for them.

There was a low level of hissing from some of the women. I agreed with him, however, and purchased his books. I really liked it when he said, "Become mean. Give your children something to remember their childhood by. No one ever brags about their parents giving them everything they ever wanted. What fun is that?"

Rosemond also encouraged us to employ play-acting as a negotiation tactic. He illustrated his point by retelling a conversation with his son who tried to excuse his low grades by saying the teacher hates kids. He told his son, "I will get the teacher fired because no one who hates kids should be working at a school." Upon hearing that, his son backed down and took responsibility for his performance.

As I listened, it dawned on me Rosemond's was pointing out that parenting could be fun if you did it right. He recommended kids have chores and be full participants in the family well-being, a process he believed the country had drifted away from since the days of the family farm when each child had his or her role and responsibilities. A light bulb went off, and I now knew what to do to relieve my tiredness.

That evening over a shrimp dinner, Nephew's favorite, I said, "Since you are living here for the year, we are now a family. You are no longer a guest."

"Okay."

"As a family," I continued, "we need to work together to keep the house and car clean since we both use them."

"I can keep my room clean the way I do at home," he volunteered.

"Well, it's going to take more than that here. Your Long Beach apartment has two bedrooms, one for you and one for your mother. This townhouse has four bedrooms and three bathrooms. We need to divide up the entire house. Since there are two of us, you can clean half and I'll clean the other half."

"You expect me to clean half this house!" he exclaimed in horror, sweeping his hand through the air towards the second-floor ceiling to encapsulate our approximate 2800-square-foot abode. "No way."

"Yes, way. Not only that, we also need to divide up the front and back yards, the car and the garage."

His mouth dropped open, and he stared at me as if I'd lost my mind.

I forged on. "Further, I'm planning to pay you an allowance. You'll get twelve dollars a week since you're twelve-years old. And when you turn thirteen, you'll get a pay raise."

The expression on his face changed from dread to a smile. "My Mom would just give me money whenever I asked for it if she had it at the time. Will this weekly money really be mine?" he asked.

"Yes," I said, nodding. "You can do whatever you want with it. You can buy your lunch at school for a dollar fifty a day or you can continue to take your lunch from the food I provide here. Obviously, if you take your lunch, you'll have more money to spend on movie tickets and other stuff you want."

"Yeah. I'll be able to meet my friends at the downtown movie theater on Saturday night. That's the happening place."

"Well, you're going to have to think about cost. With twelve dollars a week, you can buy one evening ticket, or two matinee tickets. Or, better yet, you can see twelve movies at the dollar theater. You can even afford to take a girl and pay for her ticket."

"Oh, Auntie, you're behind the times. Girls pay for their own tickets these days."

"Well, anyway, you get the point. You can also consider putting some money in a savings account."

"What's involved with that?"

"We'll open an account in your name. It only takes five dollars to open one. That way you can save money for making a big purchase, like a bike or some other sports equipment."

"That would be cool, Auntie. I think my Mom's going to send me money for a bike but I can buy something else. So, when do we begin?"

"This week," I said, pulling out a chart. "We'll divide our Saturday chores with you cleaning the living room, your bedroom and bathroom, the guest bedroom and bathroom, the car and the front yard. I'll clean the rest of the house, including my bedroom, bathroom and office, the kitchen, laundry room, garage, and backyard. During the week, if I cook dinner, you'll clean up and if you cook, I'll clean up. Does that sound fair?"

"Sure, Auntie. Let's do it. When do I get paid?"

"I'll pay you on Saturdays after you finish your weekly chores. You'll tell me how much you want to put into your savings account, and I'll give you the rest."

"Okay. That's a deal."

"Good. Here's your list of chores. Please sign here to indicate this is a contract and you will be paid for your services."

Nephew obliged.

For the first two weeks, he followed the written list and completed everything. As I counted out the dollars, a wide grin surfaced on his face.

The third week, however, he forgot to clean the living room furniture. I yelled up to him, "Nephew, you forgot something."

"Auntie, I'm on the phone with Michelle. I'll do it when I get off the phone."

Rather than argue with him, I just did the rest of his chores myself and deducted two dollars from his paycheck. When he later asked for his money, I informed him that he was only eligible for ten dollars this week.

He protested. "You should have told me you were going to do it."

"Too bad," I said. "When I mentioned that you had forgotten your chores, you were supposed to take care of them immediately and not tell me to wait until you get off the phone from talking to some girl."

"Okay," he said, grudgingly, and took the ten dollars.

The next week he forgot to clean two living room tables. I yelled up the stairs to tell him about it. "Nephew, you forgot the two living room tables. I'm going to do it for you."

"Never mind, I'll do it," he said, running down the stairs and grabbing the rag from my hand in mid-air before I could touch the table.

* * *

As kids growing up in Phoenix, Ralph and I did chores. I helped clean up after dinner while Ralph took out the garbage. One time when I didn't want to eat the peas on my plate, it caused a bit of a showdown because our stepfather Alex said I couldn't get up from the table until my plate was empty. I finally volunteered to do extra chores if I could share the peas with my collie Princess. Alex agreed. Princess was happy, and I was happier.

Ralph and I didn't receive allowances for our chores. I once asked if we could start getting money after overhearing kids at Lassen Junior High talking about their allowances. Mom and Alex both said they hadn't received allowances as kids and didn't believe in them.

I was glad to give an allowance to Nephew, however. The amount was small compared to the help I received, and I was economizing to save money to pay off the mortgage. Nephew thought it odd that we didn't have cable like he did in Long Beach, but I thought we received sufficient free channels using antennas. My cellphone was also basic, and I purchased food in bulk from Costco and stocked up on sales.

At twelve, I wasn't cleaning half the house like Nephew. After completing homework and helping with dinner chores, I spent most of my free time either reading or playing outdoors. Often, I read outdoors. I consumed so many romance novels that I detected a (Boy meets Girl, Boy loses Girl, Boy and Girl fall in love) pattern and thought I could write one someday.

* * *

A couple of weeks after Nephew moved in, I needed to fly to Massachusetts to present my research at a weekend conference, and I asked some friends to take care of Nephew for me. They agreed, and he stayed in the room with their son who was nearly the same age. After I picked him up on Sunday night, he said, "Auntie, you should have seen their house. Their kids don't do anything. Anita's mother asked her to mop the kitchen floor, and she argued because she just wanted money to go out. Finally, "Anita" did mop, and her parents gave her the money. She's lucky she doesn't live at our house. With her attitude, she'd be sitting in her room on a Saturday night."

"Well, did you offer to help while you were there?" I asked.

"Yes, Auntie," he said sternly. "I helped put away the food and I helped Anita's father clean the yard."

The next day I ran into Anita's father. "So, Terrance helped you around the house?" I asked.

"Yeah, and he also tried to help himself to my daughter," he replied.

"Goodness, she's four years older than he is."

"I told my daughter that Terrance is a player," he said. "Sherri, you need to rein him in."

Over dinner that evening, I asked Nephew if he made a play for Anita.

"She looks good, Auntie," he said, his hands forming the shape of an hour-glass figure.

"Boy," I replied exasperated. "She's four years older and nearly a foot taller than you. How were you going to kiss her?"

"I figured we could sit on the couch," he said in a matter-of-fact tone, indicating he had thought this one through.

"Terrance, if you keep this up, I won't be able to leave you with any of my friends who have daughters, except maybe "Margarita" since I know you don't like her daughter."

"Don't do that, Auntie. Maybe you can leave me with one of my friends."

"We'll see. Can you behave?"

He smiled, but said nothing for a moment before changing the conversation. "Auntie, I really like this new book I'm reading for class. It's called *Lemony Snicket's A Series of Unfortunate Events*."

"What do you like about it?" I asked

"It's about these kids who go to live with some strange relatives and weird things happen," he said.

"Oh, kind of like living here?"

"No, much worse than living here," he reassured me.

"That's good to know this isn't the weirdest place you could have moved to."

* * *

One Sunday, we visited Carmen and Florella's home. After we left, Nephew said, "Florella's room is a big mess. She has her underwear on the floor. I don't understand why her parents don't make her clean up."

"I guess that's not part of their child-raising philosophy. Florella's father thinks I've turned you into a slave because you help around the house."

"No, you haven't, Auntie. I think all kids should help clean up. The house stays cleaner that way."

"You're right Nephew, I'm glad you get it."

Days later, I spilled some tea on the hardwood floor in the living room and heard a loud scream from the top of the stairs.

"Auntie," Nephew painfully wailed. "How could you? I just mopped that floor!"

"I'm sorry, sweetheart. I'll get the mop and clean it up," I said with a lowered head. I put the tea down and retrieved the mop, with Nephew still grumbling.

I felt delighted he was taking pride in his work around the house. Score one for dividing up the chores. My energy was back.

Chapter 5

HYPOTHETICALLY SPEAKING

About five weeks after school began, Nephew brought home his first progress report. He received three B's and four C's, a 2.4 average.

I asked him, "You know what this means, don't you?"

"Yeah. I'm on punishment."

"Yep, no girlfriends, and no phone calls from girls until you bring your grades up."

"That's fine with me because I'm not interested in anyone, anyway."

His non-interest in girls lasted two weeks. On the Friday of the school dance, he asked three girls in a row the same question, "Hypothetically speaking, when I get off punishment can we hook up?" They all turned him down.

After he recounted the story over a salmon dinner, I asked him, "Isn't that like asking a woman to wait for you until you get out of jail?"

He shrugged.

"By the way, where did you pick up that phrase 'hypothetically speaking'?"

“From attending your classes,” Nephew said.

“Oh, dear, you sound like a lawyer,” I responded, surprised that all the years he sat at the back of a law school classroom while I taught had impacted him. Sometimes he had joined the conversation, such as when 10-year-old Nephew told my Entertainment Law students how he and his friends snuck into Rated-R movies during the discussion about censorship. Their ingenuity probably led to the additional security movie theaters started posting to enter the actual movie. When Nephew wanted to see Eminem’s movie *8 Mile*, I had to go in with him.

“I guess that’s what happens when you live with one,” he said.

“Did the girls understand what you were talking about?” I asked.

“Yeah, they got it, Auntie. Before one turned me down, she asked me why I wanted to go out with her.”

“What did you say?”

“I told her I thought she looks good. She’s got a great big butt,” Nephew said as he used his hands to sculpt her shape.

“Yikes, Boy, do you have to be so specific? I don’t want to hear all that.”

“Okay. I also told her I liked her personality. She then asked me, ‘What’s a personality?’”

“Goodness. Where do you get these girls from? Surely she can’t be that dumb?”

“Well, Auntie, she does look good!”

I threw up my hands in disgust, thinking *if only we could return to the days when he was terrified to have girls kiss him*. However, I said to him, "You know we basically have the same face, yet you're doing a better job attracting members of the opposite sex."

"We look alike because we both look like Grandma. Do you want some tips, Auntie?"

"No, thanks, Sweetheart. I'll feel like a loser if I take dating advice from a twelve-year-old." It occurred to me that I had slipped into calling Nephew one of the same pet names my mother called me.

"Well, Auntie, I can get the girls," he said with pride.

"When you can rack up as many A's as you do girlfriends, I'll be impressed. Now, it's time for homework," I said, pointing upstairs. "That's the only way you're going to recover girl privileges."

"Okay," he said, as he moved the dinner dishes from the table to the sink and dishwasher.

While watching him, I felt caught in a double bind. I wanted him to improve his grades, but I didn't want to deal with the phone ringing off the hook. But since learning comes first, it seemed a fair trade off. It was my idea to make having a girlfriend a privilege.

With no girlfriend on the horizon, Nephew switched his attention to his male friends. He asked if one of his friends could spend the weekend. "By the way, Kevin wants to help with the chores. Can you pay him too?"

About two inches taller than Nephew, Kevin possessed a muscular build compared to Nephew's fleshy one and skin the color of a lemon cookie, a blend of his blonde mother and his deep chocolate colored father. One of the reasons I liked Kevin was his progress report contained all A's. I hoped he could be a good influence on Nephew. "Sure," I said, "I'll make a list for three people and pay Kevin."

"Great, Auntie, that'll make Kevin happy."

After Kevin arrived, participated in chores, and left, I felt shocked by this outcome. I asked Nephew, "Why would Kevin want to clean someone else's house?"

"Well, he doesn't have chores at home. I've been telling the kids at school about my set-up. They all think it's cool."

"You're kidding!" I said, incredulously.

"Nope. Kevin even wants to negotiate a contract like mine so that he can get paid for his chores. I told him he'd have to commit to doing his work. He can't refuse to work if he doesn't feel like it. Otherwise, his parents won't have to pay him."

"What was his response?"

"He said he understood."

"Who would've thought that doing chores could become cool?"

"Yep, Auntie, you've started a revolution," Nephew said, as he tip-toed to kiss me on the cheek.

"Thanks sweetheart." *What will tomorrow bring?*

Chapter 6

SHE WANTS TO FOURTH-BASE ME

Ugh! Tofu," Nephew said one night as I served him dinner. Seated in his customary place opposite me at the dining room table, he looked at his plate in disgust.

"This is not just tofu, it's special tofu," I said with a smile. "I cooked it in a yummy sauce that my friend Orese recommended. It has soy sauce, sesame oil, maple syrup and garlic. It's delicious. You'll like it."

"I doubt it. It's still tofu," he said, rolling his eyes. "Where's a Big Mac when you need one?"

"Oh, just try it, Boy," I said, the smile fading from my face into exasperation. "Just mix it up with the brown rice and vegetables. If nothing else, it's healthy for you."

"So are your chicken and fish dishes. Why couldn't you just serve those crab cakes from Costco or that fish you bought at Whole Foods? I like those. Better yet, why don't you just make some shrimp? That's my all-time favorite," he said, rubbing his tummy.

"We have to balance our diets with different types of protein and vegetables. It's better not to concentrate on one food. Just take a bite." After he did so, I asked, "So how is it?"

"Tolerable."

"Thanks. Perhaps that's the best I can hope for. Okay, how about this? What if we save tofu until your grades drop? Then I can serve it every night for dinner until your grades come up. What do you think of that idea?" I asked, smiling again.

"No way. If I had to eat tofu every night for a week or two, I might just die."

"You won't. Anyway, how are things at school?"

"There's this nasty girl who wants to fourth-base me."

"She wants to do *what*?" I asked, not understanding the reference. *In baseball, there are only three bases. In relationships, getting to first base is kissing and hitting a home run results in intercourse. Fourth base is a new one for me.*

"You know, Bill Clinton and Monica Lewinsky," he said.

"She offered you oral sex?" I asked, astonished. "How old is she?"

"Twelve like me. She was demonstrating what she wanted to do to me with a banana."

"Stay away from that girl," I said, alarmed, while thinking *Thank you Bill Clinton. Because of you, I'm discussing oral sex with a twelve-year-old.*

"Don't worry, I will. She's nasty. All the boys talk about how nasty she is."

I felt a tad relieved, but still shocked. It was hard to believe girls were so sexually active in seventh grade. My colleague Alfred later confirmed Nephew's plight because when he took Nephew and his son to the movies that year, girls swarmed Nephew after the movie let out and explicitly propositioned him.

* * *

When I was in seventh grade, I didn't have a love life, let alone one as complicated as Nephew's. Nor did we discuss the human reproductive system in school or with our parents. About half-way through my seventh-grade year, I had noticed Mom's belly seemed to be swelling. I asked her if she was pregnant. She said no and sent me to the corner store to buy sanitary napkins for her. The next day, Mom suffered a miscarriage in the back bedroom. By the time paramedics arrived, she had lost half her blood along with her fourth child by Alex. As they carried Mom out on a stretcher, he told the paramedics he didn't know she was pregnant. "I love children," he said, as I listened from the door of my bedroom where he had sent all of us kids.

Mom was in the hospital for what felt like forever. Granny took the bus to our home after she got off work to look after us until Alex returned from his job. When Mom came back, she was not herself. It seemed like something had died inside of her along with Tony Jeffrey, the name Alex gave the baby. I didn't have time to think about how she had lied to me about being pregnant. I was worried about her.

Yep, during my seventh-grade year, the last thing I had on my mind was boys, let alone sex, and I had never even heard of oral sex. Society sure had changed.

Chapter 7

WHY CAN'T YOU JUST WHIP ME LIKE A NORMAL PARENT

Nephew had been here over two months before it dawned on me that his mother Mary and I had reversed roles. She was now the fun aunt, sending plane tickets and nice gifts, like the Louis Vuitton belt and wallet she had mailed last week. I had to instill the discipline. Yuck!

That afternoon, Nephew bounced up the stairs toward his bedroom with his pants falling below his waist and showing off his underwear. Watching him, I thought, *Lord have Mercy, I'm tired of seeing that boy's underwear.* I said, "Nephew, can't you pull up your pants?"

"That's the style, Auntie."

"Well, it's a terrible style. Nobody wants to see another person's underwear."

"People don't mind. They're used to it."

"Yes, they do mind. How would you feel if I walked around showing my underwear?" I said, as I unbuttoned the top of my pants, turned around, and slid my pants down slightly to where he could see the top of my underwear.

"Ugh," Nephew let out a long wail of discomfort.

"See, now, you do mind. Pull up your pants, please."

"Okay. I'll start wearing the Louis Vuitton belt my Mom sent me. That should help keep them up."

"Thank you."

Days later, I noticed quarters missing from the Saab's coin compartment after parking. I barely had enough to feed the meter. When I next saw Nephew, I asked him about the quarters, and he denied taking them. Since I had no proof, I let the matter drop.

A week or so passed. On television, we watched *Meet the Folks*, a reality show requiring three young men to move in with a family, which selects one of them to take their daughter to Hawaii. One of the three suitors was into pornography. The cameras captured the substantial porn collection in his bedroom closet. As part of the screening process, the family subjected the suitors to lie detector tests. On this episode, contestant Chris bragged he could beat the lie detector test because he'd been telling lies all his life.

All suitors took the test. Chris failed, but the pornography-loving guy passed as he admitted to his use. The family picked the porn-lover for their daughter's date, saying, "At least he's honest."

After the show went off, Nephew thoughtfully turned to me and said, "Let's play lie detector."

"Okay," I said, wondering where this is going.

"You go first. You can ask me any question," he said.

"All right. Did you remove the quarters from my car?"

"Yes. I did, and I'm sorry."

"How many did you take?"

"Four."

"So, you both stole from the car and you lied about it. Have you also taken money from my purse?"

"No, Auntie, I have never done that."

"Okay, Terrance, in this house you are not allowed to steal or lie. I need to be able to trust you and you need to be able to trust me. Can you understand that?"

"Yes Auntie. I'm sorry. I didn't tell you before, but that's why Michelle broke up with me. She caught me lying to her."

"Wow. You've lied to your girlfriend, too. At some point, you have to realize that lying is not a good thing to do."

"I know, Auntie. What can I do to make it up to you?"

"When you receive your allowance, you can place the quarters in the car change holder."

"Oh, I still have a few dollars left from my last allowance. I can pay the car back now."

"Okay, that's good. As for lying," I paused, "You must give up your other privileges for a week. No TV watching, no video-game playing, no telephone, no music. But you can keep your privilege to read books."

"I'm sorry Auntie, but that seems a bit much. I just got my privileges back."

"Too bad Terrance. You can go to bed now."

"Goodnight, Auntie," he said, walking over to give me a hug.

It was a hard hug to accept, as I was disappointed in him. At least the puzzle of the disappearing quarters had been solved.

Later that week, I biked to Nephew's school to help his science teacher Mrs. Schroeder sell Krispy Kreme donuts for seventy-five cents. She was raising money to fly her students to Tucson to see the Biosphere 2 project. When I heard about the trip, I immediately paid for Nephew's airfare. I had been there myself, and thought this kind of expedition could inspire him. It amazed me the friction caused by having people live in a man-made cocoon, seeking to replicate earth, or Biosphere 1.

When we didn't sell all the donuts at Jefferson, I volunteered to take several boxes to the law school, which was about a half mile away. Biking over, I balanced boxes on my handlebars. I set up shop in the Law School forum and sold glazed and chocolate frosted donuts for a dollar so I wouldn't have to deal with change. Since the Krispy Kreme Company only recently arrived in New Mexico, the donuts sold fast. As I was pedaling the sugary treats, I was struck that just last year I was dining with Kofi Annan and several other United Nations diplomats at a New York University event. My life had changed. It felt worthwhile, however, when I saw the wide smile on Mrs. Schroeder's face after I handed over more money than she was expecting to receive.

Nephew came home that evening with an equally wide smile on his face. "In seventh period, Mrs. Schroeder told everyone, 'Terrance has the best aunt in the world.' Thanks, Auntie, for helping out," he said, beaming.

"You're welcome, Nephew. Just think, I learned that I can balance three boxes of donuts on a bicycle and still ride safely." *Wow, he feels proud of me. Maybe I can do single parenthood.*

* * *

Another package arrived from Nephew's mom. This time Mary sent him a hundred dollars to buy a bicycle. She had become concerned about his walking over a mile each way to school. Even though I explained the exercise had been good for Nephew because he lost weight, she still thought he needed a bicycle. I told him we would go to Target and pick out a bicycle after church on Sunday.

On Saturday, Nephew finished all his chores except washing the car. I told him I would deduct six dollars and get the car washed at Rain Tunnel. That was fine with him. With his mother's one hundred dollars in his pocket, his attitude toward getting paid to do chores seemed to have shifted.

When Sunday church service was finished, we headed to Target. A salesman came over to assist Nephew. After he picked out a snazzy red dirt bike, the salesman helped him find a helmet and a lock so he could take the bike to school. The total exceeded a hundred and seven dollars. Between the hundred dollars his mother sent and the six dollars he saved from his allowance, he didn't have enough money.

"You'll have to get a cheaper bike," I said.

"Oh no, Auntie, I want this one. Can I clean the car and get six dollars to pay the rest?"

"Okay, but you'll have to clean it today. No monkeying around."

"Yes Ma'am."

I paid the balance and we left. On the way home, I said, "Terrance, You must follow all rules when it comes to this bike, or I'm going to return it."

"Okay Auntie."

"You must wear your helmet at all times. You must obey all road rules. If I can do it, so can you. You got that?"

"Yes Auntie."

When we got home, Nephew immediately cleaned the Saab. I told him I had to run a few errands. "I'll be back in a couple of hours," I said.

"Can I ride my bike while you're gone?"

"Nope. I want to be around when you ride your bike in case something happens."

His eyes shifted downward, disappointed.

I left.

When I drove the Saab into the garage two and half hours later, I noticed the bike in a different position and the helmet gone. I walked inside the house and noticed Nephew lying on the couch, watching television. Only yesterday did he retrieve his TV-watching privileges after the lying episode. The helmet was on the floor next to the couch.

"Did you ride your bike?" I asked.

"Yes," he nodded.

I nodded back and took items into the kitchen and upstairs to my bedroom. *At least, he's no longer lying*, I thought to myself. *That's progress. But what am I'm going to do about the bike as he's disobeyed a direct order? Why can't the boy just behave? I hate this. He keeps challenging me. If I let this go, he won't believe anything I tell him the rest of his stay here. It's going to be a nightmare.* I decided to say nothing until after dinner.

As Nephew cleaned up the dinner dishes, I said, "That's okay. You don't have to clean up tonight. I want you to go upstairs and contemplate the memory of your last bike ride."

He blinked his eyes and looked at me startled, but said nothing as he took the stairs.

I washed the dinner dishes. About 15 minutes later, Nephew came back down. "If you take the bike back, do I get my part back?"

"Huh?" I murmured, not totally understanding what he was asking.

"You know. My Mom paid a hundred dollars and I paid the rest out of my allowance. Do I get my allowance part back?"

"Yes, of course. I'll bring it to you."

"Okay," he said, and went back upstairs.

The next day, Nephew came home and saw the bike was still in the Saab where I placed it the night before. I hadn't had a chance to return it yet. He lobbied to keep the bike.

"I told my friends about the bike and they couldn't believe that I don't get a second chance. Why can't I have a second chance?"

"Unfortunately, sometimes life doesn't give second chances. Think of all the people who committed one crime and ended up in prison for the rest of their lives. I told you at the beginning that you had to obey all rules or I would return the bike. I meant what I said."

"But ..."

"No buts about it. You had your chance. Now go upstairs and do your homework. I'll call you when dinner's ready."

Over a dinner of chicken pot stickers and green beans, Nephew started again. "Why can't you just whip me like a normal parent? That's what my Mom does when I do something wrong."

"I don't believe in corporal punishment. You've known that forever. I've never spanked you. I think hitting kids just encourages them to use violence to solve their problems."

"Well, why can't you let my Mom spank me when I go home for Fall break?"

"No. You violated the rules here, not there. This is the punishment here."

"Gosh," he said in a huff as he cleaned up.

"Besides," I added, "she's been spanking you since you were two and you barely listen to her. If whippings worked, you'd have more respect for the authority of adults by now."

"That's not true," he responded.

"Yes, it is."

"Well, a spanking does only hurt for a few moments. You cry and then you get over it."

"See. Hopefully, you'll remember this for a while."

I couldn't see myself ever whipping a kid, especially one as old as Nephew. I thought of our family history. Growing up in Phoenix, I often watched my stepfather Alex beat Mom with his fists and belt-whipped Ralph while besieged by alcohol. He never physically abused me, possibly because he had other plans for my body.

I didn't want Nephew to turn out like his grandfather. It was important to model another way of behavior. *No hitting. Respect women.*

The following day, Nephew returned home from school and saw the bike was still in the car. He lobbied again to keep the bike. "You've been voted the meanest parent in the world," he said.

"Good. I'm doing my job. Now you go upstairs and do your homework."

He did as I asked, shaking his head as if he couldn't believe the situation.

I decided I needed to return the bike immediately or the lobbying would continue. At Target, I simply said to the sales assistants, "He wasn't ready for this bike."

They accepted that explanation as if they've heard it many times before.

I returned Nephew's share of the bike money when I arrived home. That night over a spicy tofu dinner, the tone of our conversation shifted.

He said, "I gave up riding my bike at home after I almost got in a couple of accidents, including one with a city bus."

I looked at him astonished.

He continued. "The bus came so close it brushed my leg. My Mom doesn't know what happened. I never told her. I just put up my bike and stopped riding."

"That doesn't surprise me," I said. "Our family has a long history of bad bicycle accidents. When I was about your age, I fell off a bicycle and cracked three teeth."

"That must have hurt."

"It did, but not as bad as what happened to my cousin Kevin. He got hit by a car while riding a bicycle and ended up in the hospital. He came close to dying."

"Wow."

"Wow is right. That's why I didn't want you riding the bike when I'm not around. I know how dangerous bicycle accidents can be."

"I'm sorry, Auntie. You were right to take the bike back. About a month before the bus accident, I got a ticket for riding my bike without a helmet."

"A ticket?" I questioned, puzzled.

"Well, it was my first warning ticket. In California, kids are required to ride their bikes with helmets. The first time the cops catch you riding without one, they give you a warning."

"Thanks for telling me. I guess you and that bicycle were not meant to be."

"I guess not. I'll just keep on walking."

"That's fine by me. Come here and give me a hug." When he came around the table I squeezed him, glad he was alive and relieved I had made the right decision. If it hadn't been for his newfound honesty, I would have never known that this boy and a bicycle were a major accident waiting to happen.

* * *

I returned Mary's hundred dollars, explaining the situation. Soon thereafter, Nephew accidentally called me Mom from the stairs and his mother Auntie while talking to her on the phone. He quickly corrected himself. I realized our roles had indeed switched. Like it or not, I was his parent for the year. It was a lot easier playing the role of the aunt. But if I could parent him in the right way, maybe I could change the dynamics of our family.

Chapter 8

HE THINKS YOU'RE FEEDING ME RABBIT FOOD

Later that week, Nephew walked in our home just as I finished a chapter for my book. Looking at him as he headed past my office to his bedroom, it occurred to me that I should teach Nephew how to cook. By the time I was his age, I could prepare several dishes. I learned from watching Granny, Mom, and my stepfather Alex. I loved watching Granny cook, but it was difficult to mimic her because of how she gave out recipes. I once asked how to make cornbread and she said you take two handfuls of cornmeal, add a handful of flour and a pinch of salt, a pinch of baking soda, and so forth. It wasn't until I took home economics in seventh grade and received recipes in precise mathematical measurements that I felt I could make some things.

Though after I screwed up a peanut butter cookie recipe by adding a cup of salt instead of sugar, my teacher recommended I get my eyes tested. Mom took me to the doctor and, sure enough, I had become nearsighted living in the turmoil of our home life.

When I next ran into Nephew in the upstairs hallway, I asked him, "Do you want to learn to cook some of the dishes we eat?"

"What, more chores?" he asked.

"This one you might like. You come from a long line of good cooks. In fact, the best thing about the time we lived with your grandfather Alex was he could cook some delicious meals. He once asked me 'Who is the better cook, me or your Mom?' I told him it was a toss-up. I liked when Mom prepared hotdogs and hamburgers, but I also liked his chicken and rice dishes. Your father is also a great cook. You might like it. Let's start this now."

"What are we having?"

"Those Chicken Pot Stickers I bought at Costco. You like those, right?"

"Yeah. Those taste great."

"Good. Come on down and let's get started." When we were standing in front of the black refrigerator, I removed the bag of pot stickers and the bag of organic green beans from the freezer. I handed them to him. "Here's the bag of pot stickers. Take out twelve – six for me and six for you– and place them in this stainless-steel pot. Add enough cold water from the faucet to cover them."

"Okay, now what?" he asked.

"Place them on the stove and turn the knob to light the gas burner and then leave the knob on high. Turn the timer to ten minutes. For the first seven minutes you'll cook the pot stickers and then you'll place this steamer basket over the stainless-steel pot and cook the green beans for the last three minutes."

"Okay Auntie, I think I get it. I've seen you do this lots of times."

After the timer sounded, Nephew finished the process. He artfully arranged the pot stickers and green beans onto two plates. We sat down at the table. Nephew had successfully completed his first recipe.

"Wow," I said looking at the artistic manner in which Nephew had arranged the pot stickers and green beans on my plate. "You've got a knack for presentation. This is delicious and it looks great. Congratulations on preparing your first meal."

Auntie Sherri's Costco Pot Stickers and Organic Green Beans for Two

In a stainless-steel pot with a steamer insert, add 12 pot stickers in the bottom, cover with a lid, and boil for 7 minutes.

Then add a cup of green beans on the steamer insert placed on top of the pot stickers.

Cover with a lid and boil for an additional three minutes.

Remove everything from the stove and place on plates.

Season with soy sauce to taste.

“Thank you, Auntie,” he said, beaming. “I think I can learn to make more things, like the juices we drink.”

“Oh, you mean the honey drinks. After dinner, I’ll show you the basic recipe and you can make your first batch.”

“Wow. I’m excited.”

“So, what do you have planned for school this coming week?”

“I need you to sign a consent form for Health Class so I can watch the videos on childbirth.”

“I’d be happy to sign. You certainly need to be informed about reproductive health. By the way, you don’t have long before you go back home to California for fall break.”

“I’m looking forward to seeing my little brother. I want to see how much he’s grown.”

“I’m sure your family can’t wait to see you, particularly your mother.”

After dinner, I washed dishes. “Remember, the general rule is if I cook, you clean, and if you cook, I clean. Does that work for you?”

“Sure Auntie. Before you clean up, can you show me how to make the juice?”

“Absolutely, Nephew. You see all this citrus fruit,” I said, pointing to a basket filled with grapefruits, lemons, limes, Valencia oranges, and blood oranges. “Pick the two you like.”

"I'll go with grapefruit and lime. I like that taste the best."

After Nephew boiled enough hot water to melt half a cup of honey, I pointed him to the electric juicer to squeeze the fruit and add it to the glass container along with enough water to nearly reach the top. He stirred and tasted his results. "Uhm, this is *good.* You should call them Auntie Sherri's Honey Concoctions."

"Okay, that's their new name. Now I'm going to wash all the dishes. You can go upstairs and do your homework."

"Sure thing, Auntie."

Wow, I thought to myself, no pushback on doing homework after I taught the kid a life skill. That was a good call.

Auntie Sherri's Honey Concoctions

(32 ounces)

Ingredients: two citrus fruits, ½ cup honey, ½ cup of steaming hot water, 16-24 oz. of cold water.

Squeeze juice from two citrus fruits: lemons, limes, Valencia oranges, blood oranges, or grapefruits. This should yield a half to a full cup (4 – 8 oz.)

Add a half-cup (4 oz.) of honey that has been melted with a half-cup of boiling water; Be sure to add enough cold water to fill the container (about 16 – 24 oz.). Stir all together.

* * *

The phone rang. I was in my study, typing the next chapter of my Art Law book. I picked up the receiver. Mr. Reynolds, Nephew's very tall Literature and Language Arts teacher, said Nephew was having trouble settling down after lunch. "Today, Terrance was bouncing off the walls," said Mr. Reynolds.

When I met Mr. Reynolds and Nephew's other teachers at the beginning of the school year, I gave them a card and asked them to call me if they ever had any problems with Nephew. This was the first.

Later that day, I discussed the situation with Orese during a Gin Shin Jyutsu session. Gin Shin is like acupuncture without the needles. She used her fingers and hands to press on the relevant points. It's very effective at balancing energy and relaxing the lucky person receiving the treatment. She asked, "What does Terrance eat for lunch?"

"He takes a peanut butter and jelly sandwich, an apple, chips, and a Wild Oats fruit bar to school."

"Sounds like too much sugar," she said. "Have you thought about giving him more protein at lunch?"

"Good idea. I eat fish in the morning," I said. "It gives my brain energy to work on my books. Do you think eating more fish will help Nephew?"

"Try it and see what happens."

That evening, I prepared tuna salad and pointed it out to Nephew. I also showed him where the blue ice packages were in the freezer to keep it cool. "You'll have to wrap the sandwich in plastic first and then add the blue ice package before wrapping everything in aluminum foil," I said.

"Do I have to eat this? I want to stick to peanut butter and jelly."

"Let's just try this for a week, Nephew. I also want you to try these organic apples and carrots. No more fruit bars for the time being."

* * *

The change worked, and Nephew settled down in school. For Mr. Kelly's science class, he agreed to sell *Human-i-Tees*, which advertised itself as "the fundraiser that makes a world of difference." Rather than go door-to-door in our neighborhood, Nephew walked to the two-story law school building, located about half mile from Jefferson. He sold a lighthouse tote bag to Professor Tim Canova, a t-shirt to former Dean Fred Hart and another one to the current Dean Robert Desiderio. If a professor was in the office when Nephew knocked on his or her door, Nephew made a sale. When his order form was complete, Nephew had sold $250 worth of t-shirts and other goods to 15 colleagues, half the staff. He had them make checks payable to Jefferson Middle School.

One afternoon, he arrived home from Jefferson to tell me that his French teacher Mrs. Dupré wanted him to bring a cake to school for a celebration. "Are you ready to test your baking skills?" I asked.

"I can bake a cake?" he asked, his eyebrows and hands rising in surprise.

"Of course. Turn on the oven to 350 degrees Fahrenheit. We'll do a simple cake that requires about five ingredients," I said, pulling out a basic cake mix, a brown egg, rice milk, butter, and my collection of organic extracts. "You get to decide what flavors you want to use to enhance the cake. I recommend vanilla and orange, but what do you think?"

"Okay. Let's try that."

As I gave instructions, Nephew stirred everything together with a hand mixer. "When can I taste it?" he asked.

"Keep blending a bit longer," I said.

A minute later, he dipped in a spoon to taste the batter. "That's good."

I gave him a sauce pan and told him to melt butter for coating the baking pan. After that, I showed him how to flour the pan and pour the batter into it. Nephew placed the pan in the heated oven and turned the timer to 25 minutes. "While you're waiting for the cake to bake, you should clean up the mess. A good chef likes a clean kitchen. It's easier to keep things organized that way," I said. "Congratulations on baking your first five ingredient cake."

While wiping up cake flour and tossing brown eggshells into the garbage, Nephew talked about his Health Class videos. "They put a tube with a camera up a woman's vagina and then filmed what happens when a penis ejaculates with and without a condom. It was nasty."

"They showed you *that*!" I said, astonished while thinking, *what did I agree to? They never mentioned this.* "I've never seen such a film," I said to Nephew.

He continued. "They also showed us the birth of a child. There was blood everywhere. I'm never having sex, and I'm never having a kid," he said, emphatically.

"Oh," I said, thinking *if that video produces this reaction, then it was worth him seeing it.*

The timer went off, and our Health Class discussion ceased. Nephew tested to see if the cake was done by jabbing a thin knife into the cake's center to see if it came out clean. When the cake was fully baked, Nephew removed it from the oven. "When can I cut a piece?" he asked enthusiastically.

"Since it's for your class, you'll have to wait until tomorrow. If you want, I'll give you a ride to school."

"Thanks Auntie," he said, giving me a hug.

The next day, Nephew returned from school excited. "My teacher *loved* the cake," he said. "She wants the recipe."

"Okay, that's easily done. I will write up the recipe for Five Ingredient Cake."

"That'll make her happy. At school, I gave a piece to my friend Kevin, and he wants to learn how to cook a few things the next time he comes over for the weekend."

"Sure," I said, hoping my kitchen won't soon be overrun with twelve-year-old boys. "Doesn't Kevin cook at home?"

Auntie Sherri's Five Ingredient Cake

Pre-heat the oven to 350 degrees.

Ingredients: (1) a basic organic cake mix, (2) one brown egg, (3) a cup of rice milk, (4) five tablespoons of room temperature butter, and (5) a teaspoon of vanilla and orange organic extracts.

Pour the cake mix into a bowl. Add 4 oz. of the room temperature butter, the cracked brown egg, the rice milk, and extracts to the cake mix. Stir.

Use the remaining tablespoon of the butter to coat the pan and add enough flour to finish the coating. Pour the mix into the pan and place in the oven.

Let it bake for 30 minutes, before testing by placing a clean thin knife to see if it comes out clean. If there is any batter on the knife, continue baking. Test again five to 10 minutes later.

One the knife comes out clean, remove the cake from the oven and place it on a rack to cool.

"Nope. I'm the only one of my friends who can cook," he said proudly. "Oh, and the kids really love those apples you bought. They keep asking for a bite."

"You're kidding?"

"No. Every time I pull one out, some kid asks me if he can have a bite of that. They like the carrots too. They say they didn't know carrots could taste that good."

"Wow!" I said, astonished.

"Yep. You're introducing kids to the organic taste. Way to go, Auntie," he said, holding up his hand to give me a high five.

I nodded in amazement.

* * *

Nephew boarded a plane for Los Angeles for his four-day fall break. By walking to and from school, he had lost fifteen pounds and no longer looked fleshy around his cheeks. Indeed, he looked fit and even cuter, if that's possible. He also grew an inch in height. "Have fun," I said, waving him off.

I had grown accustomed to his company. The townhouse seemed so quiet without him. I used the time to do some fall cleaning in the kitchen. I wiped the refrigerator and shelves. The spaces felt renewed.

When I picked up Nephew the following Sunday at the airport, he seemed to have put on a pound or two. "How was your visit with your family?" I asked.

"I thought my dad was going to have a heart attack when he saw me. He asked me, 'Is she starving you?' He thinks you're feeding me rabbit food."

"How did you respond?"

"I told him you weren't starving me, and you weren't feeding me rabbit food, but that you did feed me good food. Except for the tofu, of course."

"Of course."

"You won't believe who said she wanted to eat what I'm eating?"

"Who?"

"Kourtney."

"No way," I said. "When your stepsister visited last year, she hated the food. She wanted to leave after two days."

"Now she's gained weight and she wants to look like me."

"That's amazing."

"Kourtney sees the difference in me. Auntie, I never noticed before, but my whole family is fat, except my little brother. Everybody kept looking at me as if they were shocked. Even my best friend's mom wanted to know what I was eating. She wants you to make a list of what you're feeding me so she can try our diet."

"Wow. It sounds like I missed my calling. Maybe I should open up a fat farm to help people lose weight by changing their eating habits."

"You could, Auntie. I know my mother would sign up."

"Nephew, you look like you put on a few pounds."

"Yeah, I only ate one piece of fruit the whole time I was home. I had an apple for dessert when my dad and his family took me out to dinner."

"Can you weigh yourself tomorrow at the school gym? I'd be curious to see how much weight you gained in the four days you were away."

"Okay, will do. By the way, thank you, Auntie," he said, reaching up to kiss my cheek. "I like looking this good. I feel good too."

The next day Nephew came home from school and announced that he gained four pounds while he was in California.

"Wow," I said, "That's a pound a day."

"I know. I'm going to have to get back to eating your way. It makes a difference."

"Even tofu?"

"Yeah, even tofu."

"Good. I found another recipe. Next time, we're going to have even spicier tofu," I said with a wide grin.

"Auntie, only you would be happy discovering a new tofu recipe."

What delighted me the most was being able to connect with Nephew around food, and that he was starting to see the advantages of eating healthy.

Chapter 9

I GOT IN A FIGHT AT SCHOOL TODAY

After fall break, Nephew tried out and made the A-string basketball team. He jumped around the house as if he'd never seen a ceiling he didn't want to touch.

His enthusiasm gave me an idea. Perhaps I should link basketball to grades, to encourage him to become a student-athlete as opposed to an athletic student. The former puts academics first and the latter sports. So much has been written about the challenge of Blacks trying to make it in professional sports, especially basketball. After reading parts of *Forty Million Dollar Slaves*, I became convinced young kids would have better long-term chances of success if they concentrated on their studies.

Thinking about this information, I asked Nephew to sign a contract acknowledging that basketball is a privilege, not a right, and requiring him to obtain a minimum 2.8 grade point average on his next report card to remain on the Jefferson basketball team. If he failed to meet the above minimum grade point average, he must resign from the team or I would notify the coach that he was no longer available.

Nephew signed reluctantly, but he was convinced he could make the minimum grade point average. I reminded him that he was supposed to be aiming for straight A's so he could go to France with his French class. I had bought ice cream and baked cookies for his class to sell to make money for the trip. After I told my colleague Suedeen about all the requests for help, she said, "I used to buy brownies for a dollar so my daughters could sell them for fifty cents."

"Nephew," I said, pulling myself back to the present. "Look at these *Entertainment Books.* Mrs. Dupre wants you or me to sell these, remember?"

"I remember, Auntie."

"If I'm helping your class make money to go to France, the least you can do is earn the grades so you can go too. Don't you think?"

"You're right, Auntie. Thanks for your help. Don't you think it's great I made the team?"

"Good job. As a reward, why don't we go see a movie that I think you'll like. It's called *The Count of Monte Cristo* and is set in the late 1600s in France. You'll like the sword fighting."

After seeing the movie, Nephew seemed to like it a bit too much. When we returned from the theater, he used the broom to imitate a count swinging his sword throughout the great room, kitchen, and up the stairs. This continued for days. He appeared to be a reincarnated swordsman.

At work one day, I sold seven *Entertainment Books* to my colleagues. They liked using the coupons to receive fifty percent discounts on car washes, dry cleaning, amusement parks, and vacation packages. Driving the Saab home, I spotted Nephew walking from school. I stopped and gave him a ride. As he got in the back seat, he seemed agitated.

"What's wrong?" I asked.

He handed me his progress report, and said, "Here are my grades, Auntie."

I looked over the sheets of information. Thus far, he had received one A, three B's, and three Cs, not terribly bad at a 2.71 grade point average, but not good enough to remain on the basketball team or for a reinstatement of his girl privileges. According to our first contract, girl privileges require a 3.0 G.P.A.

"Nephew, based on this progress report, you'll have to give up basketball and girls."

"What? Auntie, I just made the team."

"Yes, and when you made the team, you signed a contract to obtain a minimum of a 2.8 grade point average. This is a 2.71. Remember, you agreed that basketball is a privilege, not a right?"

"Yeah, I remember," he said reluctantly. "There's more. I got in a fight at school today."

"A fight?"

"He pushed me, Auntie."

"Goodness, why would some kid all of a sudden push you?" I asked skeptically.

"He got mad at me because Beverly was talking to me."

"Just cause she was talking to you?"

"She's his girlfriend."

"So, you were moving in on his territory?"

"No, I wasn't. I was just talking to her. He comes over and mad-dogs me."

"You mean he gave you the evil eye?"

"Yeah. Something like that. So, I got in his face and mad-dogged him back."

"In other words, you started the fight, didn't you?" I asked.

"No, I didn't," he said.

"Yes, you did. Just admit it."

"Well, it doesn't matter because the school gave both of us TIPS."

"What's TIPS?"

"In-school suspension."

"You've been SUSPENDED!" I repeated, horrified. It sounded as if they were going to place him in solitary confinement within the school. Even though we were close to our house, I pulled over to continue the conversation.

"It's in-school suspension so we are separated from the rest of the students and have to do all our homework in a special room."

"Terrance, this is unacceptable. You didn't bring your grades back up to a 3.0 and you got in a fight. You're going to have to give up basketball as well as girls."

"Why basketball, Auntie? I just made the A-team," he protested.

"That's too bad," I said. "You've got to learn that schoolwork comes first. Before basketball and certainly before girls. If you were doing your work instead of talking to that girl, you wouldn't have got into that fight and you probably would have brought your grades up."

"Gosh, Auntie."

"Okay, enough already on this."

"Can you sign this paper for the school?" he said handing it to me. "The assistant principal wants you to know that I've been assigned to TIPS."

"Goodness," I said, taking the paper. "Let's just go home." I shouldn't have taken him to see *The Count of Monte Cristo,* I thought. The fighting has worn off on him.

That night over dinner, Nephew seemed more devastated about the loss of basketball than about anything else that happened to him that day. It was the quietest dinner with him since he arrived had three months ago. He ate and cleaned up in silence.

* * *

I empathized with Nephew. I grew up in the days where kids played "The Dozens," an insult game where you tried to be as witty as possible. Someone once told one of my cousins, "Your elevator doesn't go all the way to the top." I asked, "Did you tell him his card deck was missing his joker and all his aces?"

A typical repartee might go like this:

Child 1: You're so stupid your pickle jar is missing its salt.

Child 2: You're so stupid your pickle jar is missing its salt and water.

Child 1: You're so stupid your pickle jar is missing its, salt, water, and cucumbers.

Child 2: Your Mama!

That last statement "Your Mama" usually wrapped up the insults or led to blows.

I got in a fight once in high school when a girl cornered me in the bathroom and jumped me. She had been making snide comments about my face and clothes behind my back and within earshot for weeks. I had no idea what motivated her to talk about me since I barely knew her. However, I did notice girls from my class in the background who seemed to be egging her on. These were some of the same friends who stopped talking to me once it came out that I received straight A's on my freshman report card.

I fought back ferociously. After that, neither she nor anyone else said anything derogatory, at least within earshot. The girls seemed surprised that an egghead could defend herself.

That term applied to me in an additional manner. At the high school fair, several girls lined up to toss a raw egg back and forth. Carolyn Johnson, who looked like my great-aunt Ruth (Granny's sister), only larger and more gregarious, tossed an egg before I had a chance to stand up. It landed on my head. The girls burst into laughter, and I got nicknamed "The Egghead."

Short of an outright attack one is forced to defend, I believed Nephew would be better off in the long run if he could learn to peacefully resolve his disputes. Perhaps my International Law background was responsible for this philosophy, as I never bought the concept of a preemptive strike that some nation states argued permitted them to strike before being struck.

Later in the privacy of my home office, I questioned my decision to link sports privileges with grades. Although sports were exercise, I thought the link might incentivize Nephew to keep his grades up. I kept thinking of him as the kid who brought home straight-A's in fifth grade instead of the kid with three F's in the sixth grade. He was doing better now than last year.

At his age, I had single focused on grades because I saw them as my path out of my stepfather's home. Nephew had a different life here, and I was struggling to find the appropriate incentives.

Chapter 10

I DREAMED I JUMPED OFF THE BALCONY

The next morning, I found Nephew sitting on the floor in the living room, depressed. "What's wrong?" I asked.

"I dreamed I jumped off the balcony," he said, despondently

"Oh?"

"Yeah, my life felt useless in my dream, so I jumped."

"Did you survive?" I asked quietly, alarmed that Nephew appeared to be contemplating suicide, at least in his dreams. *Did I go too far too by having him sign the stringent basketball contract linking the right to play team sports with grades? This sport was clearly important to him.*

"No. I died," he sighed.

"Now, we can't have that, can we?" I said, as I sat on the floor besides him. "Listen, I know you're depressed about giving up basketball. I see how good you are with all your jumps around here."

"Auntie, I'm one of the best guys on the team. I could join the NBA out of college."

"I believe you, sweetheart," I said, putting my arms around him.

Terrance sobbed.

My eyes glistened. "I have an idea," I said. "Do you want to hear it?"

"Okay," he said softly through his tears.

"I've got to go out of town for work next weekend and I was planning to have you stay with my friends."

"I know."

"How about instead I send you to Las Vegas to visit Grandma and your uncle Ralph. My brother wanted to be a professional football player. Why don't you talk to him about your desire to join the National Basketball Association?"

"Do you think he'd listen?"

"Better than that. I think he would understand. He wanted to be become a professional football player and join the NFL. He played on our high school team."

"Oh. Well, it would be nice to see Grandma. She always makes me laugh."

"Okay. It's a deal. I'll get the ticket before you come home from school today."

"Thanks Auntie," he said, wiping the remaining tears away. "I'd like to go to Las Vegas."

"Go get dressed so you can walk to school. I'll see you later."

* * *

Nephew's dream scared me more than he could ever imagine. One night during my seventh-grade year after Mom returned from the hospital where she had received a blood transfusion to help her recover from the miscarriage of Tony Jeffrey, she insisted on taking her car for a drive. Alex said no, but she was adamant. "Give me my keys," she shouted at him and grabbed them.

As she headed out the door, Alex turned to me and said, "You take the kids and go with her."

I climbed in the front seat, and my brothers Ralph, Terrance, and Butch got in the back. Terrance brought his cat Coco with him. Mom drove erratically, up streets and over a bridge the wrong way. All of us kids started screaming. Mom yelled, "If you don't shut up, I'll take you out to the desert and dump you."

That brought instant silence. I felt terrified. Mom eventually ran a red light, and someone t-boned us, ramming the car. After we climbed out of the vehicle, twelve-year-old me remembered feeling a sense of relief that at least we hadn't been dumped in the desert and Mom hadn't committed suicide, which seemed to be her goal that night. She had, however, cracked several teeth when her face hit the steering wheel. Sitting in the front passenger seat, I escaped injury, but Ralph and Butch sitting in the back fractured limbs. In those days, none of us wore seatbelts. The minute the car stopped, Terrance's cat Coco leapt out the open window and sprinted away. We never saw him again, yet I couldn't fault Coco for leaving our chaotic family. When the ambulance came, we went to the hospital where Alex met us. He looked like he had been scared sober.

* * *

Remembering what happened to Mom, I vowed to help Nephew recover from these feelings. During the day, I obtained Nephew's ticket for Las Vegas. I also decided to contact the principal at Jefferson Middle School to learn more about school policies and Nephew's teachers to see how I might be able to help him become a better student. Between his fighting, low grades, and despondency about giving up basketball, I felt deep concern.

I e-mailed Mr. Reynolds, Nephew's Language Arts and Literature teacher, and thanked him for sending details indicating Nephew received a range of grades with several A's, some B's, some C's, and one F. I asked if Nephew was completing all his work assignments and whether I could meet with him to discuss Nephew's performance.

I sent similar emails to Nephew's history teacher whose detailed grades indicated zero points on two assignments, and to his math teacher, from whom he received a C despite having taken pre-Algebra in sixth grade in California. Nephew should have been two grade levels ahead of his classmates because I was told New Mexican students don't encounter pre-Algebra until eighth grade. After the teachers responded to my correspondence, I arranged to see them.

I took Nephew with me so he could hear what his teachers had to say about him. Mrs. Lopez, his history teacher, talked about him as a wonderful child with a delightful sense of humor. She said when he first arrived, the girls swarmed around him because he was new and from California. She didn't think he was used to receiving so much attention, and had a difficult time settling down and turning in his work. I asked her about TIPS.

"We have zero tolerance for fighting," she said. "All kids get TIPS on their first fight, no matter who started it. We want to encourage students to take responsibility for their anger and to resolve their conflicts using means other than their fists."

I was so impressed by what she said that I used her story to open my Albuquerque Tribune newspaper column that ran the following Thursday as the Bush Administration contemplated invading Iraq. My column headlined "Sometimes countries are in need of a 'timeout'."

Both the math and language arts teachers told us Nephew had organizational problems and did not always turn in his work. Mr. Reynolds suggested Nephew write down all his assignments in his agenda book. That way, I could check the book daily and help him track his work.

The six-foot, three-inch Mr. Reynolds also talked to Nephew about basketball and developing his mind. He told him he once wanted to be a basketball star as well, but eventually realized if he stayed in school, he'd have more options.

As we left the school, Nephew brought his notebooks and folders in his backpack. He looked toward the gym and said wistfully, "I could be there right now if only I had turned in more of my homework."

I was relieved he now saw the connection between his actions and the consequences. At home, he unloaded gobs of paper from his backpack to my office desk. One thing became clear: it was a tangled mess.

"How can you keep anything straight with all those papers mingled together like that?" I asked, looking at the mounds of paper.

He shrugged and said despondently, "I don't know."

"I'm amazed you ever turned in anything with your system. I have an idea. Why don't we go to Wal-Mart and buy you a different colored notebook for each subject? That way you can keep all your math papers together in one color and literature in another color and so forth. Do you think that might help?" I asked.

"It's worth a try. Are we going to drive or walk to Wal-Mart?"

"We'll drive in case we have a lot to carry back. Let's go now."

After parking, we walked toward Wal-Mart as I said, "You want to play a game?"

"Okay," he replied in a noncommittal tone.

"As we see people in Wal-Mart, let's guess where they buy their food? I'll point out someone and you'll guess whether they eat at Burger King, McDonald's, Subway, Wendy's, Whole Foods, and so forth. Does that sound like fun?"

"Okay, Auntie. It sounds like *your* kind of fun."

"Humor me then. I know you don't always like the healthy food I prepare, but let's see if you think it makes a difference where people eat."

"Let's go for it."

"Here's our first candidate," I said as a plump Hispanic male came into view. "Where do you think he eats?"

"Oh, definitely McDonald's," Nephew said emphatically.

"Good guess. How about that woman?" I said, pointing to a thin-ish Hispanic female. "Where does she eat?"

"She probably shops for groceries at Smith's and buys Subway or Taco Bell when she's in a hurry."

"And what do you think of that blond woman over there?"

"Oh, she's seriously fat. McDonald's, Burger King, Jack in the Box. She does them all."

"Is there anyone here that you think shops at Whole Foods?"

"Besides you, Auntie?" he asked.

"Yeah, besides me," I replied.

"Okay, I'll keep my eyes open."

The conversation ceased as we arrived at the aisle with school supplies. We picked out different colored notebooks and folders for his six classes. After going through the check-out line, we labeled them so he could recall which was which.

In the parking lot, Nephew suddenly paused and pointed, "Over there, look."

I turned as my eyes followed his finger towards a tall Black man.

"That guy looks like he's healthy," He said excitedly. "He probably shops at Whole Foods and works out too. You should date him. He could be your type."

"Thanks for the suggestion," I said. "Let's get home so we can work on your organization. The sooner you get your grades back up, the sooner you can rejoin the basketball team."

"And the girls?"

"And you can have a girlfriend again once you achieve a 3.0 grade point average. I'm not looking forward to the phone ringing off the hook, but I can deal with it."

"Thanks, Auntie."

"You're welcome, sweetheart," I said, giving him a hug. I felt as if I'd escaped a potential disaster. *Parenting is hard.*

Chapter 11

I'M GOING TO GIVE A PAAAARTY

Auntie," Nephew said over dinner one evening, "Girls really like it when I sing to them."

"Gosh, I wonder why?" I replied.

"It makes them feel good."

"I thought you didn't like singing in public. I remember the day you sang for me in the car when we were returning from the Georgia O'Keeffe Art and Leadership Camp for Boys. You said that was the first time you'd ever sang for anyone."

"It was, Auntie. Since that day, I've gotten even better. I sang for Florella on the plane when I ran into her family coming back from LAX over Thanksgiving."

"You certainly have a unique style. Why don't you sing for my December birthday party? You can be part of the entertainment, along with Goldie Garcia."

"What's Goldie going to do?" he asked, incredulously.

"She'll do comedy," I said.

"Really! I don't think she's funny," Nephew replied.

"That's cause you two don't like each other. Goldie told me you answered the phone in a deep voice. Did you tell her I was sleeping and to call back later?"

"She probably called on a Sunday afternoon and I didn't want to wake you up from your nap. You know how grouchy you get," Nephew said.

"Thanks for thinking of me. But why do you lower your voice when you answer the phone? My friends keep asking if some man has moved in."

"Cause I like the sound of my deep voice."

"Deep, it certainly is. Your voice is deeper than a lot of men I know."

"Yeah," he said, nodding proudly of this most obvious sign that he was going through puberty. "That's why girls like it when I sing to them."

"Well, you and Goldie should make a good team. She's a professional comedian who graduated from Harvard. She's played at clubs all over the country. In fact, that's how I met her. I took her class 'Stand up and Laugh' through Continuing Ed."

"Well, I hope she's funny at your party."

"She'll be fine. By the way, Nephew, I may have to go overnight to give a speech in northern New Mexico. Do you think you could stay by yourself while I'm gone?"

"Of course, Auntie, I'm old enough to stay by myself overnight."

Despite his self-assuredness, I wasn't so sure. Skepticism must have registered on my face because he put his hands on my shoulders to reassure me and said, "Don't worry, Auntie. I'll be all right."

After he left, it dawned on me that his values were evolving. When asked on a homework assignment for Health class to name ten characteristics in a life mate, he placed clean, honest, trustworthy, and generous at the top of his list, and put beautiful, good body and sexy at the bottom. When he had to draft a life plan for Health class, he said he would graduate from high school and go to college to become a doctor. I was delighted that becoming a professional basketball player, a dead-end dream for many inner-city kids, was no longer on his list. I was glad Nephew was coming to the party because my friends might enjoy meeting him.

I finalized the invitations. I decided to invite only single friends. Maybe some of them would make a connection.

I sent out the following:

You are cordially invited to a

Singles Party on Sherri's December Birthday

with comedy by Goldie,

Hors d'oeuvres by Chef Chase of the Georgia O'Keeffe Café,

and music by T

Next Tuesday, 6:00 - 9:00 p.m.

Growing up in Phoenix, while Mom and Alex didn't give house parties, Granny did and often. Our extended family celebrated the New Year, Valentine's Day, Saint Patrick's Day, Granny's birthday in April, Passover, *Cinco de Mayo*, Juneteenth, the Fourth of July, Labor Day, Halloween, Thanksgiving, and Christmas, Kwanzaa and Hanukkah.

After my half-brother Butch attended some of these parties, he questioned the celebration of other people's holidays not related to African American culture.

"Is anybody in this house Irish? Is anybody in this house Mexican? Is anybody in this house Jewish?" Butch asked.

"It doesn't matter," Uncle Charles, Granny's youngest son, replied. "We believe in solidarity with the peoples of the world."

Later, Uncle John who became the family oral historian after the death of his older brother, Bubba, explained that we celebrated Jewish holidays because we descended from the branch of the wandering tribes of Israel that meandered to modern-day Nigeria. I eventually confirmed that Uncle John had Nigerian DNA, and that my grandmother's and mother's first name (Ola) was Nigerian. Then, my colleague Rob Schwartz told me he had met Nigerian Jews. So, perhaps, Uncle John's explanation had validity.

It would take more copious research to verify Uncle Bubba's claim that we descended on other ancestral lines from Kings and Queens in Africa. He often said this when he felt the kids of my generation were acting undignified. The Middle Passage perpetrated identity theft because it cut off kidnapped people from their heritage. DNA from Uncle John and my mother confirmed that we descended from individuals who were kidnapped or sold into slavery from ancient African Kingdoms connected to modern-day Benin, Ghana, Mali, Nigeria, and Senegal. In her 2024 book *An African History of Africa: From the Dawn of Humanity to Independence*, Zeinab Badawi explored what happened to these dynasties. Someday, it may be possible to narrow DNA testing to precise African tribes and locate the Griot (oral historian) who memorized tribal history for millennia (think how often the word "begat" appears in the Old Testament).

One Fourth of July shortly after moving to Albuquerque, I had nowhere to go to celebrate. Recalling family history discussion, I figured there would be a party at Granny's house. I got in my car at 8:00 a.m. and arrived in Phoenix by 4:00 p.m. I found the family out in the backyard having a good time amidst the grapefruit and peach trees.

* * *

The wind blew fiercely the night of my December birthday party. Chase, the six-foot, six-inch chef, arrived early. We went to Wild Oats in search of fresh ingredients. He decided to make Ahi tuna wontons and some other Asian delights.

I was excited to have a genuine chef cooking for my party. I met Chase through Jackie M., the Education Director of the Georgia O'Keeffe Museum, who had started the Art and Leadership Camp for Boys that Nephew attended in the summer of 2002. Chase had cooked a delicious lunch for us at the café next door to the museum.

While Chase constructed elaborate hors d'oeuvres, I set up luminarias inside to give the great room and dining room ambiance. These brown bags contain candles situated in a bed of sand. Ron Wheeler, a library friend at work, had bought three dozen to help out a charity. When he couldn't use them, he passed them on to me. Because of the wind, if I lit them outside, their normal location, they would blow out quickly. I decided, instead, to experiment by lighting them inside next to my Black Metal Art Deco Christmas tree.

The doorbell rang and guests poured in. E.J., an Albuquerque lawyer and writer, dropped in with a gift, but didn't stay. She had another engagement to attend that night. Herb, who arrived with a bottle of wine, said he could only chat for a few moments. Fortunately, Jackie M. arrived next. She handed me a gift.

"Thanks Jackie," I said, giving her a hug. "Come in and meet Herb, the guy from work I told you about."

I turned to Herb, "I want you to meet Jackie M., my elegant, chic friend. Since you're both into the arts, I thought you might enjoy meeting each other. You two get acquainted while I put this down."

"That's a three-part gift," Jackie said. "The gray bag is part of the gift."

"Thanks Jackie. This looks wonderful. I'm going to put it down by the tree."

Jackie and Herb started chatting as the doorbell rang again. In walked Bruce, a single friend of one of my writing buddies. Bruce had agreed to play his guitar for part of the evening.

Bruce surveyed the luminarias and said, "It is not a good idea to have these inside. They suck up too much oxygen."

I looked over at the luminarias and noticed there were flames by the metal Christmas tree. "FIRE!" I yelled, rushing to the other side of the room. The new grey bag from Jackie had tipped over on top of a luminaria and lit up.

Herb, Bruce, and Jackie help me put out the fire. We then went around and blew out all the luminarias. So much for my candle-lit effect. *Thank God the tree was metal,* I thought. *A pine one would have caused even more sparks.*

The doorbell rang again, and more guests arrived. A rocket scientist friend brought his girlfriend, a young lawyer. Goldie Garcia sauntered in with a good-looking guest on her arm. "Look who I found," she said. "You remember Kenny."

"Hi Kenny. I think we met at one of the zoo concerts," I said, holding out my hand. Kenny Pushkin, a distant relative of *the* Pushkin, owned Santa Fe's Pushkin Galleries, which specialized in Russian art.

Kenny shook my hand and came in. He was followed by Steve and John, two engineer friends from the High

Desert Ski and Social Club, who brought gifts. I set them near the metal tree.

Duncan North, the screenwriter of the film *The Tao of Steve,* brought his friend Charlene. Duncan's film was about a fat guy who is highly successful with women. I guess the tall, blond Charlene proved he lived his movie.

Former Albuquerque district attorney Bob Schwartz brought Stacie, the *Albuquerque Tribune* photographer whose green eyes have led many men to ask me for her phone number. Because the *Tribune* published my column, they assumed I must know every person there.

Several months ago, Bob had asked me to invite Stacie to a dinner party so he could hit on her. When I told him she had a boyfriend who also worked at the *Tribune*, Bob said, "Well don't invite him." I declined to host the dinner. He obviously found another means of connecting with her.

Four days after 9/11, I had attended Bob's Republican fundraiser on a night that I also attended a Snoop Dogg concert. They were both new experiences for me and I wrote about the juxtaposition in my *Tribune* column titled "Snoop Dogg, Schwartz Bob: Now that's a full evening."

When I asked Bob what he and Snoop Dogg had in common, he said, "We're both known for our public speaking and occasional use of four-letter words."

After I introduced Nephew to Bob and Stacie, he declared, "That guy must have it going on." He pointed appreciatively at Bob.

"Huh?"

"Auntie, don't you know anything? For a guy like that to get a girl like her, he must have something really special about him."

"Well, for one thing he's an accomplished lawyer, not that it's any of your business. Why don't you ask the chef if he needs any help?" I shooed him off as the doorbell rang again.

Awadagin Pratt, the concert pianist, arrived with his good friend (later to become a New Mexico State Senator) Bill O'Neil. This was a rarity, I thought.

Months ago, the local gossip columnist declared Awadagin to be the sexiest man in Albuquerque after observing a long line of women waiting to receive autographed CDs following a New Mexico Symphony Orchestra concert. Awadagin greeted Chase, the chef. They said they'd played basketball together. After their chat, Chase announced he was leaving to attend another event.

Great, I thought, *we've had a fire and the chef is taking off. What else could possibly go wrong*?

About an hour into the evening, I asked everyone to introduce themselves and then Goldie began her comedy routine. I laughed, but others didn't follow my lead. They just stared.

Nephew looked over at me and rolled his eyes as if to say, *See, I told you she wasn't funny.*

I ignored his look. Instead, I introduced him, "Here's our musical guest T, who is making his debut before a large audience."

My guests clapped politely. Nephew sang the following song he wrote:

Yeah oh yeah
ooh ooh
baby
lady

verse 1

when I first saw you,
standing there baby boo
so much beauty
in your eyes
you have everything
I ever dreamed
so now I'm going to make that dream come true

hook

you are everything baby
a boy like me has ever dreamed
now it's time to make that dream come true

chorus

I want to be there
I want to go there
I want to be in your life
I love you
baby boo
Please be by my side
cause I want to be there
with you
with you

Just when I thought he was done, he chimed in with another verse:

> Many times
> I thought 'bout you
> and all the things we could do
> Baby

And then he repeated the chorus. The song felt as if it had gone on forever, but only five minutes have elapsed.

The audience clapped enthusiastically. People seemed impressed with his style. *Maybe he doesn't sound that bad, but thank God he's finished*, I thought to myself, just as Nephew announced, "Oh, I have a special one, just for my Auntie."

He crooned, "I'm going to have a paaaaarty." He sang how the minute I'm gone, he was going to invite all his friends over to raid the kitchen, drink the sodas, and eat the food. Then they'd push back the furniture, blast some rap music, and dance the night away.

The audience roared with laughter. Thirty pairs of eyes turned to stare at me just as my mouth dropped open at the audacity of this kid. I was shocked, and yet grateful he truthfully answered my question as to whether I could leave him alone at night. Now I knew I could not.

"Thank you," I said after he finally concluded. "Now, it's time to say goodnight."

"But I want to stay," he said. "I'm having fun."

"NO! It's time for you to go to bed. You've got school tomorrow. Say goodnight." I placed an arm around his shoulders to usher him upstairs.

When I returned, Awadagin Pratt came over to me and said seriously, "Sherri, you need to lock him up."

"What? If the boy had any fewer privileges, he'd be in jail," I replied.

"Well, he's a potential menace to society, at least to young girls," Duncan North chimed in.

"You're one to talk. You wrote a whole movie about how to pick up chicks."

"I'm an adult and he's a kid," said Duncan. "If you don't do something, you're going to have a real problem on your hands."

"What more do you want me to do? I have him under strict curfew. He's got to be home by 3:45 p.m. after school. I know where he is at all times," I said to both guys. Part of me can't believe that these two ladies' men were expressing alarm about my nephew. "Besides," I announced proudly, "I had him sign a contract to remain a virgin while living in New Mexico. And the contract says he can't have a girlfriend unless he maintains a 3.0 average."

Awadagin and Duncan stared at me. Their look said, *What kind of fool would think that would work.* Finally, Awadagin said, "That's it? Only a 3.0? You should have set it much higher, like 3.75 or 4.0."

"Well, it's too late to change the number," I said defensively. "He loses his privileges enough as it is."

"Okay. But you've got to give him more to do. Fill his every moment. You can get him singing lessons," said Awadagin.

"Yeah, anything to keep him occupied," said Duncan.

"Okay, okay. I get the picture," I said. "I'll look into the singing lessons. But if he gets better at singing, won't that lead to more girls?"

"Get him into sports as well," said Awadagin.

"Yeah, you've got to fill his every waking moment," added Duncan.

"Well, thank you gentlemen for your advice. By the way, Awadagin, have you met Lamia? She's a Realtor and she likes going to symphony concerts." I make the introductions and then split.

By the time 9:00 p.m. rolled around I was ready for my straggling guests to leave. I noticed the lawyer girlfriend of Rocket Scientist slipping her phone number to another male. *Not good if someone loses a relationship because of my party*, I thought. Perhaps she gave the card for business purposes, I consoled myself. However, the recipient just happened to be Eric, the tallest, cutest guy in the room. Then I noticed her walking out hand-in-hand with Rocket Scientist. I let it go, too spent to dwell on anything else.

Best of all, nothing bad happened like the time Alex took Mom, Ralph, and me to Morenci, Arizona, to spend time with his family for a Fourth of July party. Alex was drunk and angry before he even got in the car. On the way down, he constantly hit Mom and slammed her head up against the car door. I couldn't recall if she had said anything to provoke him. When we arrived at his parents' house, Alex started hitting Mom again. His family just watched as if this was a normal occurrence. Mom ran, and Ralph and I ran with her to a nearby neighbor's place. Eventually Alex calmed down and he drove us home to Phoenix that evening.

At my home tonight, there had been a fire, the chef left, and Nephew definitely made an impression. I will take this type of stimulation any day over what happened at that Fourth of July event so long ago.

Chapter 12

SHE WANTS TO GIVE ME ALL OF HER

In preparation for Nephew's return to Long Beach for Christmas, we shopped after school for presents for his family and teachers. At Walgreens, we checked out their video sales. In one aisle, we passed a row of condoms. "I need those," Nephew said.

"No, you don't," I replied emphatically. "You are not allowed to have sex. However, if you disobey this rule, you are not allowed to have sex without these. The last thing I need is to become a great aunt at my young age. You got that?"

"Yes Auntie."

"Good. While I look over these videos, you go check out those toy trucks to see if you can find one your brother might like. Afterwards, we'll go to Dillard's to find something for your parents and teachers."

He agreed.

Over a chicken dinner that evening, Nephew said he had been in touch with Kiana, his former California girlfriend. "She asked my best friend to have me call her."

"I thought you dumped her nine days after you got to New Mexico," I said, recalling the chain of people Nephew used to end their relationship.

"I did, Auntie, but she says she misses me. She wants to give me something special for Christmas," he said.

"What might that be?" I asked, trying to keep my alarm in check. *Is this why my twelve-year-old nephew was saying he needed condoms while we were walking the aisles in Walgreens?*

"She wants to give me all of her."

"Look," I said from across the table in the dining room, "When you go home, you make sure you keep your penis in your pants and your pants zipped up."

He stared at me, as if he couldn't believe I said that.

"Repeat after me," I said. "I will keep my penis in my pants and my pants zipped up."

He did as I requested.

"Now repeat it again."

He let out a hearty laugh.

"I'm serious. Nothing good can come from you having sex with Kiana at your age. She needs to keep her panties pulled up and her skirt pulled down. If you talk to her again, tell her what I said. I have half a mind to call her mother."

"NO, Auntie. Don't do that. That would be too embarrassing."

"Okay, then, you stay away from that girl."

"All right," he said, hanging his head.

."Let's wrap those presents for your teachers and family."

"Good idea. I think Mrs. Dupré will like hers," he said as his face lit up. "She has been really nice to me. I like studying French."

The next day, I put him on the airplane to Long Beach. The house felt empty without him, but I knew ten days would pass quickly. I started thinking Awadagin Pratt and Duncan North were right. I needed to give Nephew more to do. Perhaps singing lessons were the way to go.

While Nephew was in California, I cleaned the refrigerator and stove, and caught up on sleep. As I walked around neighborhood parks, taking advantage of the afternoon warmth, I realized while I had been getting on Nephew about getting B's and C's in school, I'd been operating at a B and C level in my own life. I chose mediocre guys to date and wondered why the relationships didn't work. I acknowledged I would never be happy with someone who was not smart, healthy, and somewhat spiritually aware. Just because the guy was cute didn't mean he was worth a damn.

I thought about my good-looking father John, and how Granny begged Mom not to marry him. "I could tell he wasn't any good. Just too pretty with those eyes of his," Granny told me later.

She was even more adamant about Alex. Aunt Liz said Granny pleaded and pleaded with Mom not to marry Alex. "He ain't no good. He ain't no good. He ain't no good," Granny said over and over again. Since Granny had to pick up the pieces after her daughters made bad relationship choices, I could see why she tried to ward off disaster. Three of her daughters who were abandoned by their husbands ended up boarding with Granny. Mom started a trend when we moved in after John split for Las Vegas when I was nineteen-months old. Aunt Liz had often talked about how special John's family was but what did that matter when he abandoned us.

Mom didn't listen to Granny, and Ralph and I ended up with a gambling father and an alcoholic stepfather. Mom later said she didn't know John was a gambler or Alex was an alcoholic. "He never drank in front of me when we were dating."

I didn't recall Alex ever drinking in front of us either, but he was often drunk. He must have stopped off at bars on his way home because I couldn't remember seeing beer in the refrigerator or liquor in the cabinets. *What if I inherited Mom's man-picking genes?*

Even Nephew had progressed to moving beauty toward the bottom of his list. Perhaps he could teach me something on this issue.

It also seemed as if I was underperforming with my scholarship, because I should be further along on my book by now. It's time to move my "bloomin' arse," as Eliza Doolittle said in *My Fair Lady*.

Later that week, a colleague from another law school contacted me about working on his "Art Law" text, and I proposed co-authoring. I decided to attend the Association of American Law Schools annual convention in January to help my new co-author pitch "Art Law: Cases and Materials" to casebook publishers.

Five days later at the convention, my new co-author and I met and adopted a strategy for approaching publishers. We went booth by booth to pitch our idea and why there was a need for this book. Several expressed interest and asked us to submit a proposal.

With the Art Law book now a firm possibility, I needed to separate out entertainment law cases and find a co-author for a second book. At the convention, I spotted another teacher who I knew from prior interactions had a passion for music law. I proposed we create a book focused on film, music, and television. He could draft the music section, I would draft film, and we would divide up television. He said yes, and "Entertainment Law: Cases and Materials in Film, Television, and Music" was born. He pitched it to a publisher who wanted it immediately, but I cautioned we should wait to pitch it to all the publishers when we had finished the proposal.

Now I had two books in the works. I flew back to Albuquerque with one day to spare before Nephew returned from California. Meanwhile, my scholarly agenda had doubled in size.

Chapter 13

YOU JUST ACT MEAN

Terrance returned the Sunday before the second semester began. After he walked past security, I asked, "So, how were your holidays?"

"They were fine. I got to see all my friends. They were happy to see me," Nephew said.

"How about Kiana? Did you see her?" I asked.

"No. We did *not* hook up."

"Oh, good. And did you do what I told you about your pants?"

"Yes, Auntie, I kept them zipped up. Nothing happened," he said emphatically.

"Good. How's the family?"

"They're fine," Nephew said. "They said I sounded white."

"Huh?" I asked, puzzled.

"My Mom said I was using big words now."

"What does she expect? Your vocabulary improved from reading all those books."

"Yeah, and from being around you," he said.

"There are not too many law professors running around talking as if they just escaped from Cabrini Green," I said, defensively.

"What's that?"

"A ghetto on the south side of Chicago. It gets to me sometimes when blacks think if you speak correct English, you're acting white."

"I don't think you act white," he said. "You just act mean."

"Thanks. Meanness knows no racial boundaries. I did something nice, however."

"What?" he asked skeptically.

"I cooked your favorite shrimp dinner to welcome you back."

"Thanks, Auntie. I think I put on a few pounds when I was home."

"You can weigh yourself tomorrow at school and let me know how many."

The next morning while dressing in my bedroom, I heard a big thump in the next-door laundry room. I rushed in and found Nephew lying on the cold, tiled floor. He had fainted while ironing his clothes.

"Are you okay?" I asked, kneeling beside him as he groggily sat up.

"I guess I must have fainted," he said.

"What would have caused that?'

"I drank some wine on New Year's Eve. Do you think that could have caused it?"

"You did *what*?" I exclaimed.

"My best friend and I were spending the night together, and we decided to taste a bottle of his mother's wine."

"Terrance, you drank alcohol. You're only twelve, way too young to be consuming alcohol. Your body cannot process it efficiently."

"Really?"

"Yes really. You're probably dehydrated and that increases the toxic effect. How much water did you drink while you were away?"

"Not very much, just a couple of glasses a day."

"There you have it. You know you're supposed to drink a minimum of eight glasses a day, more if you're working out. If I were you, I'd lay off the alcohol. Besides, you know your grandfather was an alcoholic, don't you?"

"No, I didn't know," he said.

"At least he drank a lot when he was married to Mom. I think he's quit drinking since then. But it's in your genes. You certainly don't want to start drinking at an early age."

"Okay, Auntie."

"You stay here while I get you some water. You'll need to drink at least ten to twelve glasses today to flush out your system," I said.

"I'll try."

"Good. Come on. I'll drive you to school and I'll make an appointment for you to see your pediatrician."

"Thanks, Auntie."

While waiting in the Jefferson Middle School parking lot to pick up Nephew to take him to the pediatrician, I contemplated the first time I tried to smoke. I was twelve and snuck a cigarette from my stepfather Alex's jacket when he wasn't looking. I went into a closet, lit up and puffed. I remembered the heat engulfing my throat right before I started ferociously coughing.

"Ugh," I exclaimed to myself at the time, "these are awful." Cigarettes immediately lost their appeal.

Hopefully fainting this morning might have the same effect on Nephew when it comes to alcohol.

After he strapped himself into the backseat of the Saab, Nephew announced, "I gained ten pounds over the holidays.

"Wow," I said. "That's a pound for every day you spent out there."

"Yeah, I didn't eat like I do here."

"Well, by now, you know what it takes to gain weight and what it takes to lose weight. The choice is up to you."

"I'm going to work it off right away. Besides, I need to start preparing for track."

"That's great. Just remember the same rules apply for track as for basketball. You have to first and foremost keep up your grades."

"Yeah, I know."

We arrived at the doctor's office. The pediatrician checked out Nephew. She confirmed my instinct that dehydration probably caused him to faint and said he should lay off the alcohol. He agreed.

***

We certainly didn't need another alcoholic in the family. One night when I was twelve, I awoke about midnight after overhearing Alex, Nephew's grandfather, arguing with Mom and trying to force her to have sex with him. She had just returned from the hospital after the car accident. Less than a month before that, Mom had been in the hospital following the miscarriage of Tony Jeffrey in the master bedroom and losing half her blood. When Mom refused him, I heard Alex say, "Then I'll go get Sherri."

I bolted out of bed and snuck out of the house. I went next door to call Granny. I told her what was happening. She said she would get Aunt Liz to drive her over. While I was waiting for them, I went back into the house and brought my brothers and sister to the neighbors to wait for Granny and Aunt Liz.

When they arrived, Alex must have heard Aunt Liz's car drive up and Granny climb out because he came to the door, holding Mom.

"Let my daughter go," Granny said to Alex. At five-foot, two inches to his five-foot, seven-inch frame, Granny felt like the emotional giant.

"No," Alex replied. "I don't have to do what you tell me."

"I've got my thirty-eight special in the car. I don't want to have to use it, but I will if you don't let my daughter go," Granny said.

Alex paused for a moment and then released Mom to a force stronger than himself. I loved Granny before this incident, but I viewed her reverently afterwards. That night, she modeled how to stand up for yourself and the ones you love.

Granny and Aunt Liz took us from our three-bedroom, one-bathroom home to Granny's three-bedroom, one-bathroom house with lots of relatives. I didn't know that night would be the last time I would ever see my bedroom or the inside of our home.

Alcoholics wreak havoc on their lives and those around them. I certainly didn't want Nephew to become one.

Chapter 14

I WAS ON TV LAST NIGHT

Nephew's first semester grades arrived in the mail. He earned a solid 3.0 and received back all his privileges. He wooed Beverly again, but kept it on the down low. The first hint came from Mr. Kelly, his math teacher, who e-mailed that Nephew had been tardy three times for sixth period math class. Mr. Kelly wrote, "He has a short writing assignment to do for his second and third tardies. As per Jefferson Tardy Policy, I will need to send referrals to the office for any subsequent tardies this grading period. Incidentally, we are only in our fifth day of the grading period."

When Nephew came home that afternoon, I showed him the e-mail. "What's this about?" I asked. "It says you've been late three days out of five this semester."

"After lunch, I walk Beverly to her class," he said.

"Beverly has two working feet. Why does she need you to walk her to class?"

"I want her to see that I care about her."

"You need to find another way of showing you care. If you can't walk Beverly to her class and get to your class on time, you need to stop walking Beverly. You are not allowed to be late to class, you got that?"

"Yes, Ma'am."

"Now, I suggest you go complete the short writing assignment and write a note of apology to Mr. Kelly about being late to his class. Explain what happened and promise that you will not be late again."

* * *

A couple of days later, Nephew said Beverly wanted to see the second *Lord of the Rings* movie with him.

"You can only go as part of a group," I said, remembering what happened when he took Florella to see the first *Lord of the Rings* movie. "Call your male friends to see if one of them wants to go. I'll give you a ride and maybe one of their mothers can pick you up. That's a long movie."

By Saturday afternoon, he still had no takers. He said he'd called friends, but no one wanted to go.

At 5:30 p.m., I announced, "I guess you'll be staying here this evening, Nephew. I'm going out to dinner. I'll see you later."

"What time will you be back?"

"I don't know. Probably around 7:30." I walked out the door and drove to the restaurant for a table for six type dinner where three single women and three single men meet for a meal. As we nibbled on desert, "Larry" asked both me and my friend Kathleen for dates. Since Kathleen and I were both looking for relationships, we felt no harm in us both going out with him. Then we could compare notes.

When I returned, Nephew greeted me. There was urgency to his voice. "Auntie, you've *got* to take me to the downtown movie theater. Beverly is waiting."

"Well, get in." As we headed down Indian School Road towards the theater, I asked, "So, which one of your friends is coming?"

Silence greeted my question.

"Who's giving you a ride home?" I continued.

Silence.

It dawned on me Nephew was pulling a fast one. I made a U-turn and headed back home. "You didn't ask your male friends to go, did you?"

Silence.

"So, it was just going to be you and Beverly at *Lord of the Rings*. You didn't even like the first one. You spent the whole time making out with Florella. You must think I'm stupid."

Silence.

"Oh, never mind. Don't answer that. You can't go. How were you going to get home? Walk?" Knowing this kid, he would have walked the three miles home in the middle of the night just so he could spend time with this girl.

When we arrived home, Nephew marched up to his room. He showered in his bathroom and prepared for bed, and I did the same thing in my rooms. After I laid down, the phone rang. "Is Terrance there?" an angry voice asked.

"Uhm, he's asleep now."

"Well, I need to talk to him."

"I really think he's asleep. Can't this wait?"

"No, it can't."

"Who's calling?" I asked.

"I'm Beverly's mother. I need to speak to Terrance immediately."

"Okay. I'll go knock on his door."

He chimed in, "It's okay, Auntie, I'm here."

I hadn't even heard him pick up the phone. I continued to listen as I wondered what the ruckus was about.

"Terrance, where's Beverly?" Beverly's mother asked.

"I think she's at the theater."

"You left her there alone?" the angry voice asked.

"I couldn't go," he said.

I added, "Terrance did not have permission to go out with your daughter to the movie theater tonight. He was supposed to go with some of his buddies, so he would have a ride home. I assumed Beverly would have been there with her friends. Quite frankly, it never occurred to me that she would be there by herself."

"I would have given Terrance a ride home," Beverly's mother said.

"I'm sorry, but I don't know you. I specifically told Terrance to make arrangements to have one of his male friends' mothers give him a ride."

"I wouldn't have left him there," she said.

"Now you tell me this, but when I asked Terrance how he was going to get home, he was silent. Not a word. The kid clearly didn't have a plan. I'm sorry about Beverly. I hope she's all right," I said.

"I'm going to have my daughter pick her up."

"I'm so sorry that Beverly has been down there by herself," I said again. "My nephew never should have arranged to meet her when he knew he didn't have permission to do so."

"Okay. I'll let Beverly know that Terrance didn't have permission," she said to me. To Nephew, she added, "I hope you won't do this to another girl. This is terrible to leave Beverly downtown by herself."

"I'm sorry," he said with genuine contrition in his voice.

After she hung up, I told Nephew to go to bed. "You should call Beverly tomorrow to apologize. Her mother was angry with you. I wonder how she'd feel if she knew you planned the whole evening just so you could suck face with her daughter?"

"Auntie, can you leave me alone? I don't feel so good."

"Sure. Have a good sleep," I said with a smile on my face. I felt like I was getting better at seeing through Nephew's shenanigans. At least he didn't lose his virginity tonight. I wondered why Beverly's mother would drop her daughter off at a movie theater to meet a boy. Didn't she know most of these mid-schoolers had gone through puberty? I sighed.

On Sunday morning, Nephew called Beverly five times. She wouldn't speak to him. He asked me to take him to Whole Foods after church. He wanted to buy Beverly some flowers.

At Whole Foods, I introduced him to a florist and explained he wanted to buy a floral arrangement, but he only had seven dollars. I left them while I shopped for groceries. When I returned, the florist had put together a gorgeous bouquet of miniature red and white roses worth about twenty-five dollars. The arrangement was so beautiful that part of me thought *where are my flowers? I should be receiving this bouquet for putting up with Nephew's escapades all these months.* I thanked the florist. To Nephew, I said, "How lovely. She really hooked you up."

At the register, the cashier rang up Nephew's purchase based on the $5.50 tag the florist attached. As the cashier scrutinized the bouquet, he said to Nephew, "Wow, someone in floral must really like you."

"Thanks," Nephew replied. "She was *really* nice."

"SUPER NICE, if you ask me," the cashier responded, sarcastically.

The next day, Nephew left for school with flowers in hand. I departed about ten minutes later to walk to the law school. I passed by Montezuma Elementary School, which had just experienced a tragedy. Carolyn Rustvold, a 28-year-old occupational therapist at the school, had been murdered. The school was in mourning. There were camera crews outside. I saw them and thought what a horrible situation.

Back home that evening, I asked Nephew, "How did it go with Beverly?"

"I had to wait for lunch time to see her, and my teachers and friends kept asking me who the flowers were for. When I finally saw Beverly, she wouldn't speak to me at first. But when I gave her the flowers, she smiled."

"Hopefully, she'll forgive you."

"I hope so too, Auntie."

After Nephew returned home the following day, he raced up to my office just as I finished working on a chapter for my *Art Law* book. "Auntie," he said, breathlessly, "You'll never guess what happened?"

"What happened?" I asked, noticing he could barely contain his excitement.

"I was on TV last night," he said excitedly,

"What?" I said, puzzled.

"My friends saw me on the news. The TV showed me walking with my flowers as I passed by the school."

"Wow. I guess they must have thought they were memorial flowers for Carolyn Rustvold, the teacher who was killed. It's been all over the news."

"I guess so."

"Congratulations on your first television appearance. It's too bad they didn't stop and ask you who the flowers were for."

"I was on TV," he said, ignoring my comment. "Can you believe it? I have to call my mother."

"Go ahead," I said. "You began the month of January by fainting and now you end it by being on TV. Only you, Nephew. Only you."

He practically skipped to the phone as I returned to work.

I paused for a moment and rejoiced at another moment of happiness in our home.

* * *

For Mom, my siblings, and me, moving into Granny's house brought relief to be away from Alex's violence. My brother Ralph and I wanted to continue at our schools. By then I was in seventh grade at Lassen Junior High School and he was in fifth grade at Valley View Elementary. Because Mom's car had been wrecked, she couldn't take us. We initially got rides to school from our pastors, Sister and Brother Burdick. I had been teaching Sunday school at their Foursquare Church for a long time, and Sister Burdick had given me piano lessons so I could play for some of the church services. The song lyrics, "Blessed Assurance, Jesus is Mine," wafted through my brain as I remembered the small church in South Phoenix.

After a month, the Burdicks said they could no longer take us. Granny then taught Ralph and me how to catch the city bus to the closest drop-off point. From there, we walked a mile and a half to Lassen and Ralph continued for another half mile to Valley View. Our walks in those days bore similarity to the one Nephew took to Jefferson.

Ralph and I enjoyed meandering through neighborhoods to get to school. On the way home, I would often stop at the public library to check out books. Eventually, I started volunteering to help re-shelve the romance section. The advantage to me was that it gave me first pick from the ones just returned.

I was glad Nephew was experiencing memorable moments of attending school in Albuquerque, just like I did in Phoenix.

Chapter 15

TWO WEEKS

As Nephew reconnected with Beverly, I met Dick, a tall entrepreneur, for drinks. After we became acquainted at a fundraiser for an arts organization, he invited me to have cocktails at a downtown bar. We chatted and he seemed charming. As he left to catch a plane, he said he would call when he returned.

"Fine," I said, thinking this one had possibilities. "I look forward to it."

The next day, I spoke to the arts coordinator about our next big function. As a board member, I liked to occasionally check in. As the conversation wound down, I suggested she send Dick a ticket since he helped with our last fundraiser.

"Oh, he's already on the list. I plan to invite him and his fiancé."

"*Fiancé*," I repeated, attempting not to sound as shocked as I felt.

"Yeah. I think she travels between Albuquerque and back East somewhere."

After our conversation ended, I checked my AOL account and discovered an e-mail message from Dick.

He wrote of how much he enjoyed meeting me. "A real delight, in fact." He concluded by suggesting places where we could dine when he returned.

I looked at the email time and noticed Dick's message came in just as the arts coordinator was telling me about his fiancé. That's synchronicity, as Carl Jung would say. I was clearly meant to know the truth about Dick before I spent any more time with him. I didn't respond. Darn. My relationships were lasting about as long as Nephew's. I had to hand it to him, though. If one of his dalliances fell through, he just moved on. *Next!*

February dawned in Albuquerque with bitter cold temperatures and clear blue skies. People often confuse Arizona and New Mexico, thinking they are both just desert. Not all arid regions are the same, however. Situated in high desert, Albuquerque is approximately 5500 feet above sea level, whereas Phoenix can be found in low desert at about 1000 feet above sea level. In August, Albuquerque temperatures hover between 95 and 105 degrees Fahrenheit while Phoenix can exceed 120 degrees. The winters also diverge in temperature. While it frequently snows in Albuquerque in December, I remember seeing snow flurries only once in Phoenix as a child. Ralph and I were astonished and tried to catch the snowflakes with our tongues.

On a windy morning, Nephew announced he was going to help Mrs. Dupré, his French teacher, after school. "She asked me to help her with a homework assignment, and," he paused for effect, "I said yes."

"Great," I said. "I'm sure she appreciates the help." I'm glad Nephew had found more things to do other than girls. After Kiana wanted to give him all of herself, I asked if anyone knew of a singing teacher at our Neighborhood Ladies Lunch at the end of January. One neighbor recommended someone at her church. I called for an appointment for Nephew, thinking about the advice of Awadagin and Duncan.

Later that day, Mrs. Dupré called to determine whether Nephew would be going on the French trip. Alas, I told her it didn't look like he'd have the grades to go. "By the way," I said, "Terrance told me this morning he planned to help you run a homework session this afternoon. How did it go?"

"He popped his head in, said hello, and left," Mrs. Dupre said.

"He didn't stay?" I asked.

"No. He just left." She said.

"That's odd. He made such a big deal this morning about saying he was going to help you."

"He didn't."

We said our goodbyes, and I was left to wonder where Nephew was after school today. He told me one thing and did another. *What does it take to get through his head that I need to know where he is at all times? These one-week punishments don't seem to be having much of an impact. Should I ground him for the entire month of February?*

When he came home, I confronted him. "Where were you?" I asked. "Mrs. Dupré called today about the French trip."

"I went to play basketball," he said, realizing he was busted.

"With whom?"

"With the boys. They were practicing for the championship. You can call them if you like."

"Okay, I will. Get the phone numbers."

After he did as I asked, I talked to the mothers and their sons. They confirmed Nephew played basketball after school. Later as I served chicken, brown rice and broccoli for dinner, I announced he was grounded for two weeks for misrepresenting where he went. "You should go to the school library tomorrow to get something to read. You're going to be spending a lot of time in that room of yours," I said.

"Two weeks?" he asked, incredulously.

"Yes, two weeks. Perhaps you should pick up more of those *Lemony Snicket's A Series of Unfortunate Events* books. You like those. Fortunately for you, you will get your privileges back by President's Day. You will spend that weekend with Lisa and her son Mark while I attend a wedding in Santa Barbara."

With his head down, Nephew climbed the stairs to his bedroom. What serendipity that his teacher call today. I must have been meant to know where he really was. The Universe seemed to be conspiring to prevent him from getting away with anything.

Valentine's Day approached and in a reversal of dating fortunes, Nephew had no girlfriend and I had two dates. I met both men through attending table-for-six type dinners for single folks. I first heard about these dinners from a law school classmate living in San Francisco. When an acquaintance mentioned there was something similar in Albuquerque, I signed on and met "Larry" and "Sam" at two separate dinners. Both invited me out for Valentine's Day dinner, but I planned a trip to Santa Barbara on the actual day.

Larry, a financial planner, asked me to join him for dinner at the Artichoke Café on the Thursday before Valentine's Day for an early celebration. He arrived with a bouquet of roses and I gave him a box of chocolate-covered strawberries from the Candy Lady, an Old Town Albuquerque institution.

Regrettably, Larry didn't make a reservation at the Artichoke Café and the place was packed. He suggested we go downtown to Conrad's, about a mile from where we were.

We walked toward his car pockmarked up with dents. He asked me to wait a moment until he got in, explaining the passenger door only opened from the inside. Once we were both seated, Larry said, "I bought this old Saab at a charity auction and it needs some work."

"Oh, I hope the heat works. It's awfully cold tonight."

"Unfortunately, that's one of the mechanical defects on my list to get fixed."

"All right. Why don't I drive?" I offered. "It's cold outside with snow on the ground."

He agreed and we got into my Saab. I immediately turned on both seat-warmers, a Swedish invention I adore. Lord knows, I purchased my share of bad cars. My very first was a lemon-yellow colored Subaru I bought at an auction without driving it. When I went to pick it up, they had to jump start the engine. I should have left it on the lot to be re-auctioned, but I drove it off only to have it die again. When it quit working in the middle of Phoenix's red-light district, I gave up and had it junked. My third car, a Datsun B-210, functioned with only two cylinders. It could get up to 50 miles per hour on a steep downward slope. I was a graduate student at Princeton, and a German friend nicknamed it the Dream Machine. He had been driving an old Mercedes on the Autobahn when it blew up. He looked over the Datsun and said it should last the year. When I sold it in May the night before commencement, we toasted the Dream Machine with Champagne.

After being seated at Conrad's, a restaurant with linen tablecloths and fine bone china in one of Albuquerque's oldest hotels, Larry ordered paella for two. It arrived in a cast iron pot overflowing with tasty seafood. We talked about Larry's life and how he came to be in Albuquerque. It seemed he had at least one failed marriage. He asked me, "Would you ever give up total control over your life to another person?"

I stuttered, "Uh, no. Why would anyone want to do that?"

He mumbled something about life being easier when someone else made all the decisions for you. If he meant the reverse, I couldn't see many women wanting to be responsible for him. After all, he's an adult.

I thought about Larry's car without functioning doors or heat and wondered what kind of idiot would let him make any, let alone all, decisions for her.

Fortunately, the waiter arrived with the check and broke the awkward silence. Larry removed his credit card from his wallet and placed it on the tray without hesitation. The waiter took it away. I thanked Larry for a delicious dinner.

A few minutes later, the waiter returned. "I'm sorry, Sir. Your credit card has been declined."

"Did you run it through again?" Larry asked. "Maybe something's wrong with your machine."

"Yes, Sir, we ran it through five times and each time it came back declined. Do you have another card, Sir?"

"No. I'm sorry I don't."

"We always take cash, Sir."

Larry pulled out his wallet and looked at its empty folds. "I'm sorry. I don't have any cash on me."

"Wait, here, Sir. I'll talk to the manager."

After the waiter left, Larry explained he just deposited money on his card yesterday. "There should be plenty of money available on the card," he said.

"What kind of credit card requires you to deposit money first?" I asked.

"The kind for people with debt," he said without blinking.

"But aren't you in the finance field?" I asked, feeling like I was in a bad-date dream.

"Yeah. I just started about six months ago. I'm trying to dig myself out of debt after my last divorce and this pay-as-you-go credit card seemed like it would help."

"But why did you choose such an expensive restaurant?" I asked.

"Well, it's not like I could have invited you to McDonald's for Valentine's Day."

I fell silent, afraid if I spoke some terrible words might spill forth. I vowed to neither pay the bill nor wash dishes. Larry got himself into this mess and he could get himself out.

"Sir," the waiter called for Larry's attention. "The manager agreed that you can come back tomorrow and pay the bill."

"Thank you. Tell the manager I appreciate his accommodation," Larry said smugly.

"Okay, we can go now," I said, eager to escape. When I dropped Larry off at his car, I didn't even look at him. "Thanks. Goodnight," I mumbled.

"Can I see you again sometime?" he asked.

When it snows in Phoenix in August, I thought, but said, "You can always call. I'm off to California this weekend."

"Have fun," Larry said and exited.

I drove away. *Lord, have mercy, as Granny often said. What a knucklehead. The saving grace was that the meal tasted good and the flowers were beautiful.*

Sherri with Nephew at age 1

Mom and Sherri with Nephew at age 5

Sherri with Nephew at age 7 in Hawaii

Nephew in kayak in Hawaii

Justice Ruth Badar Ginsburg joins Sherri and Nephew at the University of Hawaii Law School

Baking cookies with Wally "Famous" Amos

When Sherri met President Bill Clinton, they discussed Hope, Arkansas, where he and Sherri's mother were born.

Jefferson Middle School
Albuquerque, New Mexico

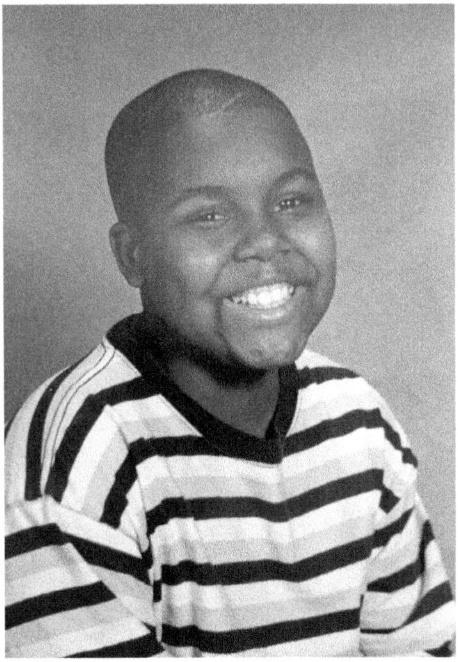

Nephew at age 11, before he moved in with Auntie Sherri.

Nephew at age 12 while attending Jefferson Middle School, seven months after moving in with Auntie Sherri.

Chapter 16

I WOULD HAVE DUMPED HER ON THE SPOT

The next day Nephew went to stay with friends, and I jetted off to California for a Valentine's Day wedding. The bride and groom couldn't have picked a better setting for their ceremony. I could see why the Spanish colonial buildings and beach-front area had led people to nickname the Four Seasons Santa Barbara as the wedding place for the stars. Dolphins jumped in the background as Matt and Stephanie exchanged their vows. The sound cut out, but no one seemed to care. The setting luxuriated bliss as the sun seeped into the distant horizon. The wind blew softly as I retreated into the beauty of the moment.

At the reception, Stephanie, in her Vera Wang gown, said she felt grateful the ceremony sound system was her one wedding glitch. The silence made the two of them feel alone in their idyllic surroundings. The waiters served a multi-course dinner that charmed the eyes and satiated the palate. Then dancing began. This event must have cost Stephanie's doctor father, whose beauty queen second wife seemed close to Stephanie's age, a small percentage of his fortune.

Someday, perhaps this will be me walking down the aisle with a wonderful man in spectacular environment and enjoying a festive reception. My mind returned to reality when I remembered Dick's fiancé and Larry's bouncing credit card. It could be a while.

* * *

Upon returning to Albuquerque from Santa Barbara, I picked up Nephew who had fun with Lisa and her son Mark. Lisa smiled as she talked about what a joy it was to have Nephew stay over. "They played video games, and we had pizza. Terrance said he doesn't get pizza too often at your place."

"He told the truth on that one," I said. "Did he tell you about the huge zits he gets on his nose right after he's consumed pizza?"

"No. He didn't mention that," Lisa said.

"He wouldn't, I guess. Thanks for having him."

A day later, Sam called to confirm our date. We agree to meet at a Thai restaurant. The five-foot, seven-inch Sam was plump and gregarious. He sported a full head of hair, unlike the balding Larry. Sam was also a world traveler. We talked about the places we'd experienced. When the bill arrived, Sam picked it up and said, "I never know what to do in these situations."

"You invited me," I reminded him.

"Right, I should pay, then." He pulled out his wallet, paid with cash, and we ended the evening pleasantly enough. He invited me and Nephew to go skiing the next weekend. He made it clear we'd have to pay our own way, although he said if we had the *Entertainment Book*, we might get a discount.

"That sounds like fun. I bought the *Entertainment Book* to help my nephew's French class," I said. "I'll talk to Nephew about it." We shook hands as the date ended.

After several phone conversations, Sam and I realized we were incompatible, so we dropped the idea of a ski date.

A few weeks later, Nephew and I were driven to the Santa Fe ski resort by Rocket Scientist, the friend who had attended my December birthday party with his lawyer girlfriend. He had proclaimed himself a top-tier black diamond skier.

At the resort, Nephew and I both signed up for lessons, he for snowboarding and me for skiing. It would be more accurate to say I went ski plunging.

In mid-afternoon, our class advanced to the chair lift. We exited at a low level. As I took off, I started screaming as I realized I was heading toward a giant tree.

"Fall! Fall!" yelled the instructor.

After I did as commanded, I later caught up with the rest of the class. As I arrived, the instructor told the class, "She's an example of why screaming doesn't help. If anything, it only makes you go faster."

On that note, I decided to quit skiing while I was still alive.

I ran into Rocket Scientist. He gave me some instructions on using poles. Our teacher had told us not to use them.

"They actually help," Rocket Scientist said.

Nephew soon joined us. He looked exhilarated, although I notice him rubbing his left wrist.

"How was your day?" I asked Nephew.

"It was great. I went all the way to the top," he said pointing up to the highest mountain.

"You did *what*?" I asked. Nephew's had chutzpah. I barely made it through one chair lift session.

"Yeah, I wanted to try the highest slope," he said.

"How did it go?" I asked.

"I fell," Nephew replied.

Rocket Scientist chimed in, "I gave him some tips on how to get down the mountain."

We decided to call it a day and head back to Albuquerque. As we passed mountain scenery to the right, I again noticed Nephew rubbing his wrist in the backseat. "What's wrong?" I asked.

"I fell on my wrist," he replied.

"How is it?" I asked.

"He should be fine in the morning if you ice it when he gets back," Rocket Scientist said.

"Were you there when it happened?" I asked.

"I came up afterwards and helped. He held on to my pole while I pulled him down the mountain," said Rocket Scientist.

"Were you going to tell me about this?" I asked Rocket Scientist.

"Not unless it was necessary," he said, glancing at Nephew through his rear-view mirror.

"This sounds like a conspiracy of male silence to save his ego," I said.

"I don't know about all that," Rocket Scientist replied. "I'm sure Terrance will be fine after a day or two. If his wrist starts to swell, then you'll need to take him to the doctor."

"Thanks," I said. "How's your girlfriend?"

"She's no longer my girlfriend, thanks to *you*!" he said irritated.

"What do you mean thanks to *me*? What did I have to do with it?" I asked.

"Your party," Rocket Scientist said matter of factly, as if those two words told all.

"What did my birthday party have to do with it?"

"She met him at your party. If not for your party, she'd still be my girlfriend," Rocket Scientist said.

"You brought her to the party, and you knew it was a singles party," I said.

"Yeah, well, I didn't expect her to meet someone else," he replied.

"Why did you bring her?" I asked.

"It sounded fun and we were dating. The worst thing is that he and I shared a loft during a Taos ski trip."

"That must have been interesting. Was Girlfriend there?"

"No, she didn't make it," Rocket Scientist said.

"That would have been awkward. Sorry it didn't work out. Thanks for taking us skiing, and for pulling Nephew down the mountain." Given how mad Rocket Scientist was about losing his girlfriend to another friend of mine, I was surprised he spent this much time with Nephew and me. I guess he wanted to get what happened off his chest.

At home, Nephew, who had listened to the entire conversation, added his two cents worth. "If my girlfriend had tried to pick up another guy at a party that I took her to, I would have dumped her on the spot."

"Sounds like Rocket Scientist didn't know until later," I said.

"Still, what Girlfriend did was low," Nephew said.

"You and Rocket Scientist seemed to have bonded."

"Yeah, he was nice. And he helped me out without telling you. He's cool."

He went to ice his wrist, and I thought about how much I was learning about the male psyche from being around him. At twelve, he was already a man's man, and a ladies' man.

Chapter 17

I'M BORED

Nephew was after Beverly again. Over a stir-fried chicken dinner, he announced they were an item.

"She loves me," he said proudly, holding his hands over his heart.

"Great. However, she's not allowed to give you any special gifts, like all of herself," I said.

"Don't worry, Auntie. Beverly's not like that."

"Let's hope."

"She's also smart. She got six A's and one F," he stated proudly, as if to announce he had finally found someone brilliant.

"What did she get the F in?" I wondered.

"I don't remember."

"Okay. You went through a lot of trouble to get with Beverly. I hope it lasts."

"It will, Auntie."

"You want to place a bet?" I asked.

"No. That's okay."

"Well, you seem to be doing better than your Auntie when it comes to dating."

"Why do you say that?"

"I went out with this one guy, and his car had no heat and his credit card bounced."

"Too bad he didn't speak to me before taking you out," said Nephew, all knowing.

"Why?" I asked.

"I would have told him to get his act together first, because you're finicky," he said.

"My sister Vera uses that word," I said.

"She's right."

"Okay, Mr. Dating Expert, what would you say about a guy who turned out to have a fiancé?"

"What do you mean?"

"I meet him. He asks me out. We go out for drinks. The next day, he e-mails me asking for another date just as I'm talking to someone else who tells me that he has a fiancé."

"Ooh, he's busted! Did you e-mail back?"

"No. What could I say? Will your fiancé be attending, too?"

"Well, you could look at it this way, Auntie. You're so fine he forgot he had a fiancé."

I laughed. "I should be paying you to live here and have dinner with me. Spring Break is almost here. You'll be going home in a week. Any plans?"

"Just to see my family and friends."

After I placed Nephew on a Southwest Airlines flight back to Los Angeles, I cleaned the house. I read Karen Kingston's little book called *Clear Your Clutter with Feng Shui* and implemented its suggestions. I donated old clothes I hadn't worn in two years. I piled books that had been gathering dust since college into the car to take to the library. The house was shining when Nephew returned. I was glad to see him.

The next afternoon, I picked him up from school, which was a rarity since he usually walked. "You need a haircut," I announced while running my hand over the top of his head. "Weren't there barbers in Long Beach?"

"Yeah, but I'm letting my hair grow out," he said.

"You're *what*?"

"I want an Afro."

"No, you don't. What you need is a military cut. I think you'll look great bald."

Nephew gave me that look, the one that said he thought I'd lost my mind.... "No, Auntie, I don't want to be bald."

"Yes, you do, sweetheart. You'll look fabulous. It's the in-thing."

"How about a shadow fade? Auntie, you think I look nice with a shadow fade."

"That was before Spring Break. Now I think you're going to look wonderful bald, with that nice military edge," I said, driving towards the barber shop. "In fact, let's get your hair cut right now."

"No, Auntie. How about a shadow fade?"

"Here we are." After we walked in, I told the barber that Nephew wanted a military cut.

"No, my Auntie got it wrong," he said to the barber. "I want a shadow fade."

"Well, what's it to be?" the barber asked.

"Oh, darn," I said, reluctantly. "I guess he can have a shadow fade. It's his head, after all."

"Yes!" Nephew screamed, throwing up his fist triumphantly.

"I'll be back," I said, as I exited quickly. I needed to get out before bursting into laughter. The shadow fade, with its soft edges around the sides, was the haircut I liked best on him, and he played right into my hands. I remembered John Rosemond saying parenting could be fun if you were willing to engage in a bit of playacting. If I had suggested a shadow fade, Nephew would have fought for an edge so he could grow an Afro. *There's nothing like a little reverse psychology to get the kid to do what you want.*

"You look handsome," I said, after picking him up.

"Thanks, Auntie, for taking me to get my hair cut."

"You're welcome, sweetheart."

"Auntie, did you know the barber likes you? He kept asking me about you."

"Yeah, I know. I let him trim my hair once, and he asked me out while his scissors were snipping away."

"Did you say yes?"

"I thought, hmm, there could be a wrong answer to this question. If I said 'absolutely not, you're too fat,' he could have left me bald."

"You said yes, then."

"I said something along the lines like maybe one of these days when you're no longer my beautician, because I can't date my beautician. He seemed to buy it."

"That's probably why he wants to ask you out now because he no longer cuts your hair."

"Yeah, but he trims your head. What if he got mad at me and nicked you?"

"I don't think he'd do that."

"Perhaps you're right."

By week's end, Nephew announced as we ate red lentil soup for dinner, "I'm bored."

"With what?"

"Beverly."

"You're joking?" I threw up my hands in amazement.

"No, I'm not. It's not fun anymore."

"How long have you two been together?"

"Three weeks, if you count Spring Break."

"That's the longest any of your relationships have endured. You got together the week before Spring Break, you go home, come back, and a week later you're ready to call it quits. Too bad, I didn't put any money on the longevity of this relationship. I could have won another dollar."

"Auntie, don't make fun of me."

"Terrance," I said holding up my fingers. "First, she rejected you, saying you're too short. Second, you got yourself suspended after fighting over her. Third, you endured the wrath of her mother when you stood her up. Fourth, you got in trouble with your math teacher for being tardy when you walked her to class. Finally, she becomes your girlfriend. And, you're bored. How can that be?" I continued.

"It's just not fun anymore," he said.

"So how are you going to break-up with her? Do you know her best friend?"

"Naw. I'm just going to ask her if we can be friends."

"Okay. Hopefully, that'll do it. Let me know how it turns out. The world wants to know."

After Nephew went upstairs to do homework, I pondered his relationship with Beverly. It occurred to me that he had just demonstrated something that had perplexed women for ages. *Why do men lose interest so quickly after women admit to loving them?* Males enjoy the thrill of the chase. Look at Rocket Scientist. His girlfriend misbehaved and he yearned for her. Nephew obviously received more pleasure from pursuing Beverly than from capturing her. If she had agreed to date him in August, the relationship would have ended in August. But she refused, and he pursued until he won her heart in March. Then he became bored.

* * *

When I was Nephew's age, I kept too busy with my classes and extra-curricular activities to think much about boys. It was Mom's idea that I attend a Seven Sister college. When we first met with my high school guidance counselor, Mr. Horowitz, Mom proudly told him, "She's a straight-A student and she's going to Radcliffe or Vassar."

Mr. Horowitz made sure that I was tracked into gifted and advanced placement classes in high school so I could be prepared. Mom's idea became my dream as the Mount Holyoke College representative took me under her wing. She would later proclaim me her greatest discovery for our *alma mater*.

Chapter 18

DON'T SCREAM

Beverly bit the dust, just as sports resurfaced in Nephew's life. His grades in order, Nephew tried out and made the track team. I told him all the basketball contract rules applied to track. He must keep up his grades to remain on the team.

I attended a track meet to see Nephew run. He was fast, but his friend Kevin was faster. I couldn't help but wonder why Kevin didn't get born into my family and become my nephew. Kevin was a straight-A student, and he liked working around the house. Of course, God works in mysterious ways as Granny often said. If Kevin had been my nephew, I probably wouldn't feel that I was living in a movie most of the time. And, Nephew made me laugh.

"I'm going to Taos this weekend," I told him after the track meet. "Who do you want to stay with?"

"Kevin."

"Fine. I'll ask Kevin's mother if it's okay." Kevin's mother readily agreed. She seemed to like Nephew as much as I liked Kevin. She thought Nephew fun, and I liked the seriousness of her son. She said that Nephew could come home with Kevin after school on Thursday.

After Nephew left for school that Thursday morning, I headed to the Taos Talking Pictures Festival. I had a press pass to write about the event for my *Albuquerque Tribune* newspaper column. After the premier movie showed, I met Eva Amurri. When I saw her name on the screen, I couldn't believe my eyes. I'd been showing a Robert Mapplethorpe photo of her in my Art Law class for ages. Ms. Amurri confirmed that she was, indeed, in the photo.

The next day, I spotted her in the lobby of the Fechin Inn, a renowned Taos resort. I explained that I was so thrilled to make her acquaintance because the nude photo of her toddler-self clutching her private parts had caused quite a stir among law students over the years. Some viewed it as innocent and others thought it borderline child pornography. She assured me that it was quite innocent. "Mapplethorpe used to photograph my mother. I would tag along. I liked taking my clothes off, so he snapped me."

I was so engrossed in *resolving* the mystery of Eva Amurri that I didn't notice the red- headed woman standing next to Eva was actress Julia Roberts. She was wearing very little makeup and seemed only five-foot, four-inches tall instead of the towering model type I had imagined her to be after watching *Pretty Woman*. From behind Amurri I heard another woman announce, "It's time to go." Amurri stepped aside, and I glanced down to see Susan Sarandon staring up at me and noticed Goldie Hawn in my peripheral vision. I found out later from another journalist that Susan Sarandon was Eva Amurri's mother. They left, and my mouth dropped open. I was too shocked to speak. I decided to write my next *Tribune* column about being in the presence of celebrities and only knowing their mystery.

On the way back to Albuquerque, I got pulled over by a cop about twenty miles north of my home. He clocked me driving the Saab ninety-two miles per hour in a seventy-five-mile zone. Over dinner, I told Nephew what happened, and explained that I would have to go to court. "When adults do wrong, we sometimes have to face a judge," I said.

"What happens?"

"The cop will probably testify that I was speeding and there will be a mini trial," I said. "I'll let you know the outcome."

* * *

Terrance blurted out over dinner one evening, "All my friends think you're mean."

"Why?" I asked. "What did you tell them?"

"Nothing," he said, shrugging.

I guess I was supposed to think his friends reached this conclusion out of the blue. It seemed kind of an odd statement given that a month ago Nephew achieved a 3.0 on his third-quarter report card and received all his privileges back, including the right to do sports and have a girlfriend. I hoped we'd turned a corner and he would keep up the good grades.

The next afternoon I was in my study working on my *Art Law* book when I heard the door opening downstairs. I descended the stairs to find a distressed-looking Nephew in the kitchen.

He looked at me as he held something behind his back and said, “Don’t scream. Just give me my extra chores. But don’t scream.”

“Fine,” I said. “Did you get an ‘F’?” I assumed it was his progress report causing his anguish and decided to start the questioning with the lowest grade possible.

“No.”

“A ‘D’?”

“Times two,” he stated matter of factly.

“Ahhhhhhhhhhhhhhhhhhhhhh!” I screamed.

“See now. You said you wouldn’t scream,” he said, calmly as if he was the adult and I was the kid.

“Give me that paper, Boy,” I said, reaching out to grab it because I was required to sign it.

As I looked over his Language Arts grade, I noticed six zeroes or F’s on various assignments. I said, “You’re back to not turning in your work. How much more basic can this be?”

“What’s my punishment?” he asked, ignoring my question.

“I don’t know. I need to think about it. Go upstairs and do your homework.”

I returned to my study until it was time to prepare dinner. When the meal was ready, I called him down.

Over supper, I announced that he had to give up his television, phone, girl, and athletic privileges until he brought his grades back up to at least a 3.0 average. I now wondered if the statement about my being mean the night before was a set-up to lighten the punishment he knew was on the way.

Nevertheless, I was beginning to think it didn't pay to yell and scream at him. I had to get better at imposing punishment. When I screamed, I lost. It was as if the boy got the better of me when my temper flared. When I was calm, I won.

At Jefferson Pride Night, an annual event celebrating the achievements of the school's students, I saw Mrs. Dupré. In addition to being Nephew's French teacher, she was also one of his track coaches. To my surprise, she backed me up. She said I was right to make him quit track until he brought up his grades. She told Nephew that he needed to work on his homework because he could do both. He needed to learn to manage.

Later, I heard her tell another teacher approvingly, "She has him right under her thumb."

If only it was true, I thought. *Keeping this kid heading in the right direction is an ongoing struggle.*

Another person I ran into at Pride Night was "Nicky," the mother of "Moredus," one of Nephew's basketball buddies. Nephew once said over dinner that she was as mean as me. "I hear you're tough," I said.

"You have to be to keep up with these boys," Nicky replied.

"Terrance tells me that Moredus can't receive calls from girls."

"Yeah, that's right. Girls are not allowed to call my home. He can call them, or he can give out his cell number. He can't give out the house number."

"You're my hero," I told Nicky.

Terrance and Moredus walked up. "Nicky is my hero," I said to them.

Terrance rolled his eyes. Moredus shook his head. They walked away muttering something under their breath. I imagined they thought that an unholy alliance of the Mean Mothers Club had just been formed.

Good fortune struck Nephew at Pride Night. One of his friends gave him a dirt bike, the low rider of bicycles. This one was so small that his knees touched the handlebars when he rode it sitting down. I confirmed the friend wanted to give the bike rather than sell it. The friend told me he had just received a new one and Nephew could have this one. With rundown tires, it looked like it was on its last legs. We placed it in the Saab's trunk. I told Nephew that he still had to follow all bike rules.

With his next allowance, he bought new plastic handles and paint to spruce up the bike. He made it his own.

Two weeks later, I went to court for my speeding ticket. I ran into a former student who asked if I was there to represent someone. I wiggled my way around why I was in the building. I was too mortified to acknowledge that I was at a courthouse to defend myself.

In the courtroom, my name was called, and I found myself in a booth with a lawyer who did not know who I was. She offered me a plea bargain. Since this was my first offence, I could plead guilty or no contest and be sentenced to traffic school. If I completed traffic school and remained ticket-free for six months, the ticket would be expunged from my record. Thinking this was probably the best deal I could hope for, I plead no contest. She told me to sit outside and the judge would call me.

About fifteen minutes later, my name was summoned. The judge asked me if I understood that I had the option to go to trial.

"Yes, your honor," I said.

"I probably don't have to read you your rights," she said, obviously recognizing me from my role as a law professor.

"No, your honor, you don't," I said, feeling embarrassed to be a defendant. It was bad enough when I ran into the former student on the way into the building. "I accept the plea bargain."

She signed the paperwork. The clerk handed it to me. I went downstairs and paid the fees for traffic school. They gave me a report date.

On the day of traffic school, I dressed conservatively and drove to a building situated on the campus of the St. Pius X High School, which was co-established by one of my neighbors Josina Baca Chimenti and her former husband Joseph. While Nephew thought some of my neighbors were weird, not all the nearby folks fit in that category.

That morning, there were about a dozen of us attending the session. The instructor asked us to introduce ourselves and state why we were there. As we revealed our offenses, there was only one other guy there for highway speeding. The rest were there for driving without a license, driving without insurance, failing to pay prior tickets, and not obeying stop signs. From this small sample, it appeared more poor people ended up on the wrong side of the law. Were they stopped more often? I didn't know.

As the day wore on, I felt glad to be here. The teacher was pleasant, even as she showed videos of deadly car accidents. The phrase "to scare straight" came to mine as I watched the carnage.

As she reviewed the traffic laws, I learned things I didn't know or had forgotten in the two decades or so since I first took my driver's test. She explained the rules require a reckless driving ticket for speed exceeding ninety-five miles in a seventy-five-mile zone, and the police officer had the option to arrest the speeder. I became relieved that the cop had clocked me at ninety-two. Since I bought the Saab, I'd noticed that I couldn't always feel how fast I was going by the reaction of the car. Unlike my previous small SUV, the old un-air-conditioned Rocky that shook once the needle hit seventy-six, the Saab seemed to run smoother at high speeds. Once I had glanced down and found myself going a hundred. I vowed that it was time to master cruise control, once and for all.

That evening over a dinner of salad with chicken on top, I told Nephew about traffic school. "Adults face consequences for their bad behavior, just like kids," I said. "Only sometimes we have to confront cops and judges."

"You actually look happy," he said, surprised.

"Yeah, I'm glad I went. I was driving too fast. I have to slow down, and I'm going to master cruise control. I'll make you a deal, Nephew," I said.

"What kind of deal?"

"How about you following all traffic rules on your bike and I'll lower the Saab's speed to legal limits?"

"Okay," he said, extending his hand for me to shake it. After we shook hands, he added, "By the way, when I'm sixteen, can I have the Saab?"

I rolled my eyes. He wanted a car that I just got into trouble driving. "No way," I said. "When you turn sixteen, you're getting an old Volvo. That way, when you crash, both you and the car will survive."

"But I don't want an old Volvo."

"If you're living out here, you do because that's going to be your only option. One of my friends bought her son a Saab and he totaled it. Fortunately, he walked away with barely a scratch. Then her husband bought their son another Saab and he crashed that one too."

"He's lucky you're not his mother. You would have had him catching the bus after the first accident."

"Yeah. Imagine two of them!"

"I'm not worried about accidents. My Mom said she's going to buy me a brand-new car."

I contemplated whether having a new car would stop him from having an accident. One of my friends had sons that had crashed two used Saabs. I didn't think the age of the vehicle was as important as the experience of the driver. "That I want to see," I said to Nephew. "Only a fool would trust you with a new car. And I don't think your mother is a fool."

"That's what she said," he replied.

"We'll just see when the time comes. If you're living out here, you're going to have to get a job, save your money, and buy your own car."

"What?"

"Yep. All my friends who bought cars for their kids have wreckage to show for their generosity."

"Not all kids get in wrecks, Auntie."

"Many do, especially brash sixteen-year-old boys. That's why they have the highest insurance rates. Some of my friends are paying several thousand dollars a year to insure their teenagers. That's another reason why you'll need to get a job, to pay your own insurance."

"You're mean, Auntie Sherri."

"I know, Sweetheart."

Two weeks later while driving home from work, I spotted Nephew paused at the crossing light on Indian School Road. He was dutifully waiting for the light to turn green so he could bike across. He was wearing his helmet, but the strap was unbuttoned.

When he arrived home five minutes later, I said, "I saw you on your bike and you didn't have your helmet buttoned."

"I had my helmet on," he said. "What's the problem?"

"You know what the problem is. What good is a helmet that is not strapped on? If you get hit, it could go flying off your head and you'd suffer brain damage."

"Oh, I didn't think about that."

"Isn't that the problem? When are you going to learn your lesson? You were nearly hit by a bus in California. Give me the keys to the lock," I said calmly.

"What are you going to do?" he asked, defiantly, "You can't return it to the store, and you don't know the boy who gave it to me."

"Yeah, but I know how to lock-up the bike," I said.

"When do I get it back?" Nephew asked.

"Later," I said.

"Later? When's later?"

"Later is when I say so. Now go do your homework. You're just an accident waiting to happen."

As he stomped up the stairs, I said, "You might as well master the safety rules around this bike, or I'll also be selling your car when I catch you driving without a seatbelt. You won't even have a chance to get into an accident."

He shook his head and muttered, "Mean! Mean! Mean!"

I headed out to the garage to lock-up his bike for the time being. It was too bad I couldn't send him to traffic school to watch movies about bad bike accidents. Then maybe he'd take the safety issue seriously. The best thing about handling this incident was that I remained calm.

Chapter 19

THOSE VULTURES WILL SWARM

Easter arrived, and I felt like a derelict because I forgot to buy Nephew an Easter basket. I'd become thoroughly exhausted. We did make it to church, and I enjoyed the service. On the way home, I listened to Nephew chatter about all the girls at church who liked him. I just hoped none of them had our phone number.

Easter reminded me of happier times with my family. The holiday brought church singing, new clothes, Easter baskets, egg dying, and egg hunting. I remembered Mom and her sisters Liz and Gussie shopping for a dress for me when I was fifteen. The three of them grabbed the same pink one off the rack at once.

That dress ended up doing double duty because I wore it to Grandpa's funeral after he died in December 1976. It was a grand affair as ministers from all over the country came to say goodbye. Grandpa had initially joined the clergy when the family lived in Hope, Arkansas. His father had been an undertaker who also preached funerals. Because Grandpa had severe asthma, he moved the family to Phoenix in the late 1950s. He ended up pastoring churches primarily in the southwest, including Arizona, New Mexico, Texas, and southern California.

Granny would periodically visit him, taking me and my cousin Yolanda with her. Granny liked to arrive early to the bus station, sometimes as much as three hours before our departure. Yolanda and I thought that was awful to wait so long for our bus. If we complained or squirmed, however, Granny would pinch us. Uncle John declared that we were lucky since when he was young, Granny used to bite him. After hearing that, Yolanda and I quit complaining. Better a pinch than a bite.

Ralph, the oldest of my brothers, called two days after Easter to say his first son arrived on Easter Monday. Another nephew! I was thrilled for my brother, but I didn't anticipate volunteering to take in this one.

* * *

In one month, my freedom to come and go as I pleased would be returned. Since I was on sabbatical from my university job, I should have felt refreshed. Instead, with Nephew as my only student, fatigue engulfed my body.

In a few days, Nephew would turn thirteen, and I was debating what to do for a surprise. Over a salmon, brown rice and salad dinner, I asked him what he wanted for his birthday.

He responded, "Can Kevin spend the night and go to Hinkle Family Fun Center with me on Saturday?"

I agreed. The Hinkle Family Fun Center had laser tag, bumper boats, miniature golf, and several fun games. Since his actual birthday was on a Wednesday, I e-mailed Mr. Reynolds, Nephew's language arts teacher, to ask if I could bring a cake to his class to surprise Nephew. Mr. Reynolds consented.

On the day, I showed up with a cream-cheese cake and ice cream puffs, courtesy of Costco. Mr. Reynolds' other students saw me before Nephew did. When he looked up, an expression of sheer delight appeared on his face. His classmates sang "Happy Birthday" as Nephew grinned wider than the Rio Grande. They gathered around as I parceled out the cold sweet treats.

After the bell rang, I suggested to Nephew, "Why don't we take the leftovers to your lunch period."

"Those vultures will swarm around like there's NO tomorrow," he replied.

"Well, we've got over half of it left. Since it's a cream cheesecake, it'll spoil in a few days. We might as well give it away."

"Okay, Auntie, but I warned you."

I took the cake to the lunchroom, and kids descended from every direction. They asked me who the cake was for. I pointed to Nephew. Even though many of them didn't know him, they asked for pieces.

While Nephew served his friends, I cut smaller pieces for the other kids.

He came over and said, "See, I told you."

"Oh, well, maybe you'll make some new friends."

As we stood there, one boy whom I had met before through his law-student mother came up and said to Nephew, "So, it's your birthday?"

"Yeah," Nephew replied.

The boy handed him a dollar and said, "Happy Birthday."

"Thanks," Nephew said.

After the boy walked away, I said to Nephew, "See, you got an extra birthday gift."

"Okay. You're the best Auntie in the world. Did I tell you I love you?" He placed his arm around me, hugged me, and planted a big kiss on my cheek.

"You're not so bad yourself, Nephew. Most of the time."

He smiled.

"See you back at the ranch," I said, thinking maybe this will be the incentive that gets the kid to take his grades seriously. After all, there was only a month left.

That evening, Nephew brimmed with happiness. I realized I did the right thing to execute a surprise party in addition to Saturday's event.

* * *

My mind jetted back to the unexpected surprises that our father John was constantly springing on us. Mom had taken Ralph and me by Greyhound bus to visit John in Las Vegas. I had marveled as the lights of the city came into the distant foreground and at how happy John looked when he picked us up at the station.

He took us to meet his new wife Lula Mae and new son Michael. I felt we had been replaced.

Years later in the Phoenix County Clerk's office, I found the petition for divorce and judgment of divorce ending John's marriage to a Lula Mae on October 21, 1971. The petition said they had been married in Las Vegas, Nevada, five years earlier, just before our family visit in 1966. Interesting, clause III of the divorce petition said "[t]hat there have been no children born the issue of this marriage." Thus, the Michael that John had introduced to Ralph and me as his son must have been Lula Mae's child before she met John.

According to the fifth clause of the divorce petition, the defendant Lula Mae "has been guilty of excesses, cruel treatment and outrages toward the plaintiff; and that said conduct of defendant has made the continuation of this marital relationship unbearable to plaintiff." *What could Lula Mae have done to John?*

John had filed the divorce petition on August 25, 1971. The divorce was granted less than two months later. Talk about a quickie divorce! Lulu Mae did not appear, and the Court determined that, based on the evidence, "all the material allegations of the Complaint are true." I found it disturbing that both Mom and John were married to abusers at the same time, she to Alex and he to Lula Mae.

In 1973, John picked up Ralph and me from Granny's house to introduce us to a new set of people in his life. We walked into his home and there sat a woman with a newborn baby. "Surprise," John said.

"This is my new wife Annie and my new son Jonathan." I felt my face drop. *How does John keep getting married and having children when he doesn't send child support to take care of Ralph and me?* After Ralph and I said hello to John's new family, we soon left.

That same year, I went on my first date to my high school Christmas Prom as a freshman. Before the date, John dropped by Granny's house. He told me that I looked nice and then urged me not to do anything rash. Uncle Charles added to the warning, "One night can ruin your entire life."

My date was a senior and I felt thrilled that he invited me. Mom bought we a white evening gown with a navy-blue polka dot top. As we were dancing at the prom, my date asked me to marry him. "I want to have a dozen children."

I stopped dancing. "Take me home," I demanded.

When my date drove up to Granny's house, I barely said goodbye before I sprinted like a cat being chased by a dog to safety. He terrified me so much I didn't go on another date until I was about to graduate from high school.

Thereafter, Mom often said, "Don't get married until you can support yourself." I became determined to graduate from high school with honors, do well in college, and go to law school. I planned to become a lawyer because, like on the *Perry Mason* show, I wanted to solve a crime, that of my missing siblings.

Realistically, I knew there was nothing I could say that would scare Nephew away from girls. Better to just continue creating an open relationship so at least I know what's going on with him.

Chapter 20

YES, AUNTIE, I DID IT

As Nephew walked toward the front door on Friday morning, the last day before his big bash on Saturday at the Hinkle Family Fun Center, I asked him, "Did you finish all your homework?"

"Yes, Auntie," he said heavily.

"Well, did you finish your paper for Mr. Reynolds? He was so nice to let me give you a surprise party in his classroom."

"Yes, Auntie. I did it," he said.

"That's good. I'm driving to Santa Fe to drop off the Saab at Smart Motors to have the air conditioning repaired," I said. "Have a good day. I should be back home by the time you and Kevin get here."

After he closed the door, I got in the Saab. As I drove to Santa Fe, I thought of the irony of having bought the car for its air conditioner, only to have it go out. I probably would have been better off paying to put an air-conditioning unit in the Daihatsu Rocky. The thousand-dollar cost was the same and I wouldn't be out of pocket for what I paid for the Saab. Nor would I have been caught speeding since the Rocky couldn't go over seventy-six miles per hour without shaking.

When I returned to my university office in a Saab loaner car later that morning to work on my *Art Law* book, I checked my computer inbox. Mr. Reynolds wrote that Nephew turned in a paper today with two sentences.

"Two sentences?" I wrote back, astonished. "I just asked that scoundrel this morning about your paper and he said he did it. I'll deal with him when he gets home."

I was beside myself. *How could the boy regress like this? I replied with confidence to the teacher, but what do I do? I thought we had turned a corner and he would behave better. This behavior must be corrected, but what should I do about his birthday event at Hinkle Family Fun Center and his friend Kevin spending the night? How do I teach Nephew that his schoolwork comes first?*

I discussed this dilemma with several people at work. Pat Trainer, the registrar, suggested punishing him on Monday. My colleague Alfred Mathewson said, "There's a reason that God made kids biologically connected to parents so we couldn't return them when they do something ridiculous."

Fortunately, I had an appointment to see Orese for a Gin Shin Jyutsu session for the early afternoon. Today, I needed the energy-balancing touches of healing, as my nerves felt fried. I explained what happened and Orese and I debated strategies.

About an hour after the session, I called Kevin's mother. I explained that Nephew had a situation to correct before Kevin could spend the night. Thus, the sleep-over was canceled until Nephew could correct his problem. If he did, I'd pick Kevin up around noon tomorrow for Hinkle Family Fun Center and he could spend the night on Saturday. In the meantime, I asked her to bring Nephew home.

When he walked through the door, I handed him Mr. Reynolds's email. "Here," I said. "Read this."

Terrance did as requested. "It wasn't just two sentences. It was three," he protested.

"Whatever!" I said, as I resisted the urge to roll my eyes. "The fact remains that you were supposed to turn in a full page. Now because you are in dereliction of your duties, I want you to write two pages and it has to be typed. You got that?"

"Fine," he said, with his face looking like thunder.

"You have two choices," I continued in an even-toned voice. "Your sleep-over tonight is canceled. You have until noon tomorrow to rectify this situation. I want to see a typed two-page paper and you have to do all your chores. This house had better shine. Otherwise, we're canceling Hinkle Family Fun Center and Kevin can't spend the night."

"Okay," he said and walked up to his room. He closed the door behind him.

I didn't know what to expect. But I didn't have time to think about it as I had to return the loaner Saab to Smart Motors so I could get my car back. The entire trip to Santa Fe and back took about two and a half hours.

When I returned, Nephew handed me a two-page typed paper. "Here," he said. "It's all done."

"Thanks," I said, surprised. I read it and there were no typos or spelling mistakes. As I glanced around, it became clear that Nephew was half-way done with his chores. "It's getting dark now. Do you want to wait and mop tomorrow?"

"Oh, NO! I'm going to finish tonight," he said emphatically.

"Okay," I said. "Carry on."

"By the way," he asked. "What's a scoundrel? Mr. Reynolds said you called me one."

"Here," I said, handing him a dictionary. "Look it up."

He let out a chortle as he read, "a disrespectful person, a rascal."

He returned to cleaning. Given how fast he was moving, one might think there was a fire under his behind. When I had told his mother Mary about the situation earlier today, she had suggested I whip him. That was not my style. I was getting results with my tactics. I didn't even have to raise my voice.

I went up to my room. I felt like jumping up and down because I didn't scream. I calmly laid down the law and the boy responded. Hear, hear to successful parenting moments!

Chapter 21

WHAT ARE YOU DOING GOING THROUGH MY TRASH

"What are you doing?" I asked Nephew a week later after noticing him standing over a wastebasket in the hallway outside his bathroom.

"I'm emptying out my backpack. I decided to clean it out," he replied. "These are just old papers from the semester. I'm cleaning up to go back home. I have less than a month left."

"How many of these papers received A's and B's?" I asked.

"Ninety percent," he said without hesitating.

"That's great." I left him and went about my business.

That night, I popped up from a dead sleep. I felt disturbed. I went to Nephew's bathroom and retrieved the garbage can from under the sink. I looked through his papers. While there were A and B papers, there were also C papers. Then my eyes noticed a paper that received 90 out of 150 points. "That's a D," I said to myself as I read over his cursive script:

> *...I was sick when I came out of my mother's womb. I was a sick baby, but I am a wonderful child today. My life story is a fantastic story. I want everybody to know about it.... I lived in a horrible neighborhood. I lived in Long Beach, California, a city where you have to duck from bullets. I lived a pretty hard life. I think that people are behind me. There are gangs walking around with guns, trying to find somebody to kill. If somebody lived my life, they would know how it felt to be a little black boy.*

After reading this paper, I shifted from feeling dismay at the D grade, which I now understood given the grammatical errors, to concern that he had ducked bullets in California. Then I wondered if he had made up the story. I decided to return to bed and quiz Nephew about the paper in the morning. I left all his papers on the banister outside my bedroom.

Around 7:00 a.m., I heard him turning on the water faucet in his bathroom. "Terrance," I called out. "Can I talk to you?"

"Sure Auntie. What's up?"

"I found these papers in your wastebasket," I said pointing to the pile.

"What are you doing going through my trash?" he asked.

“I wanted to confirm your statement that 90% of your papers were A’s and B’s. Anyway, I found this D paper for Language Arts. Tell me about this passage,” I said as I read the part about ducking bullets. “When did this happen?”

“It happened on the way to school in Long Beach.”

“Terrance, you live in a nice neighborhood. I’ve walked through your neighborhood. I’ve never seen gang members walking your streets with guns out looking for someone to kill.”

“Auntie, it happened when I was going to school from my best friend’s house.”

“Well, I’m going to call your Mom. She needs to know you’ve been dodging bullets on your way to school.” I picked up the phone and dialed Mary’s number.

“Is that really necessary, Auntie?” he asked.

“Yes, it is.” I was now totally suspicious of the story.

She answered after one ring. “Mary,” I said, suddenly remembering that it was around 6:00 a.m. in California. “Sorry to call so early.”

“What’s wrong?” she asked, sounding slightly alarmed.

“I found this paper that Terrance wrote for his Language Arts class. In the paper he says he dodged bullets in Long Beach.”

“What? That never happened,” she replied emphatically.

"When I asked him this morning, he says it happened at his best friend's house."

"His best friend lives in a nicer neighborhood than we do. Put Terrance on the phone."

I handed the phone to Nephew.

He took it reluctantly, looking at the receiver as if it was a snake about to bite him. "Hi Mom," he said.

I heard only his side of the conversation, consisting of a string of apologies.

He dejectedly handed me the phone. "My Mom wants to talk to you again."

I took the phone from him. "Hi, Mary," I said.

"I told Terrance that the day he survives a drive-by is the day we move. I don't know why he made up that story, but it's not true. It didn't happen in our neighborhood or near his best friend's home."

"Thanks for clearing that up, Mary." After I put the receiver down, I turned to Nephew. "I'm going to call your father and let him know too," I said to Nephew as I dialed my brother. After I got him on the phone and explained the situation, he asked to talk to Nephew as well.

Nephew handed the phone back and said, "I'm sorry, Auntie, that I made up that story."

"Well, sorry doesn't cut it. Now I've got to e-mail your teacher and let him know that you fabricated that story in case he needs to deduct more points since you didn't write a true-life story. Okay, get dressed and go to school."

That morning I e-mailed Mr. Reynolds and asked him if the project was supposed to be truthful. He replied that he didn't mind if students use their imagination in writing stories. What he cared most about was that they write.

I repeated Nephew's fantastic story to three Anglo colleagues at work. They all expressed concern that he had to go through such a bad experience. I then explained that he made it up.

When I told my African American colleague, Alfred Mathewson, about Nephew's story, he said immediately that it was hogwash. "One of my daughters went through this period when she wanted to be from the ghetto, too."

"Gosh," I said. "What is it with black kids these days? It's as if they think they are not black unless they are ghetto black."

"It's too bad, isn't it?" Alfred said. "Black kids are not content to be middle class. They are having an identity crisis."

"You know what's interesting," I said, "You immediately knew Terrance's story was BS, yet the Anglos didn't. They assumed it was true. It's sad to find black kids are buying into the same stereotypes. They believe they are not really black unless they're dodging bullets or having a terrible life."

"It's a shame, isn't it?" Alfred said.

"It's too bad there are not role models for middle class blacks. Even when the media tries, like with *The Cosby Show*, people think it's unrealistic," I said.

"It's an uphill battle to get black kids not to buy into stereotypes about blacks."

"Now, black kids are creating the stereotype stories themselves. I guess I'm in for some more conversations with the Bullet Dodger when I get home this evening."

After talking to Alfred, I went back to work. When Nephew came home, I was there to greet him with a big grin on my face. "So did you dodge any bullets on your way home from school today?" I asked from the top of the stairs.

"No, Auntie."

"Are you sure? Come here. I want to make sure there are no holes in your shirt from where the bullets barely missed you."

"That's okay."

"Are you really sure, Terrance? I want you to show me how you duck when the bullets are flying by," I said moving my head about.

"Oh, Auntie," he replied, exasperated. "Leave me alone."

"Oh, come on now. Show me your ducking moves. Let's pretend the bullets are flying now. I want to see you dive for cover," I said, laughing uncontrollably.

Nephew walked right past me into his room and closed the door.

I returned to my study and put in another hour and a half on my book before descending the stairs to prepare dinner. When dinner was ready, I called up. "Hey, Bullet Dodger. It's time for dinner."

Nephew slowly came down. "Why can't you let it go, Auntie?"

"Oh, come on. I want to hear more about your life as a little black boy."

He sighed as he walked to the table.

"Terrance," I asked seriously, "How often have you told this bullet-dodger story?"

"Just to a couple of kids at school. I said I'm sorry, Auntie. Why can't you let it rest?"

"Well, I'm wondering why you'd want people to think you live such a horrible life?"

"I don't know, Auntie. The kids kept asking me about California and I just told them what I thought they wanted to hear. When I told stories of California, they gathered around. I became popular."

"But what are you going to say to them when they come over for your going-away party in a few weeks? Then they are going to see how you really live."

"I'll just tell them that this is how *you* live."

"But, Terrance, this is how *you* live while you're here. And when you're in California, *you* live in a decent home. Your Mom's apartment is nice and clean. She takes good care of you. You don't lack for food or clothes. Stories like the one you wrote reflect badly on your parents. It sounds like they don't love you enough or they are too poor to live in a decent neighborhood."

"Well, Auntie, I never thought about it like that. Anyway, I'm going to stop telling that story. Can't we give it a rest?"

"I just want you to be able to accept your life as it is."

"Okay, Auntie, no more bullet-dodging stories. Can we change the subject?"

"All right. So what girl are you after these days?"

He smiled. He was back in familiar territory where he didn't have to make-up his life.

* * *

As a kid, I didn't have to make up any stresses in my life. I remembered when my seventh-grade year ended, and we were living at Granny's house. We celebrated when my brother Butch turned five in June, and my other brother Terrance turned six in August. We happily had his birthday party in Hermosa Park. It felt like we were free from the nightmares perpetrated by stepfather Alex.

About a week later, Alex showed up unexpectantly at Granny's house and announced he was taking Terrance, Butch, and Vera (who were six, five, and two) on a vacation to California before school started. Mom agreed. Ralph and I packed their bags. We kissed and hugged them.

When our siblings didn't come home after two weeks, Mom called Alex's relatives who said they didn't know where he was. Our home mysteriously caught fire and burned a month later. Mom was able to retrieve a few of our belongings.

She soon suffered a nervous breakdown and was hospitalized. When she recovered, she got a nursing job at Doctor's Hospital, and divorced Alex. Mom was awarded full custody of their three children, but that court order was meaningless when they were missing.

Decades passed before our half siblings told Ralph and me that Alex drove them to California in a U-Haul cabinet, with their belongings in the back. Alex told them, "I'm taking you on vacation."

Our brother Terrance now liked to joke, "I've been on vacation for most of my life."

As a child living at Granny's, *Perry Mason* became one of my favorite TV shows because the lawyer always solved the crime. I vowed to learn the law and determine what happened to my siblings.

By the time I turned sixteen and Ralph fourteen, Mom had suffered several mental collapses over the loss of her children. She became so despondent she was no longer able to work and care for Ralph and me. After Ralph got into trouble, he went to live with our father John. By then, John had progressed from frequenting other people's gambling establishments to opening his own. It became known as the Gambling Shack.

I went to reside with Mrs. Reid who was Mom's social worker and a foster care provider. Alex's actions led to all five of us losing our mother.

I focused on my studies, and obtained a scholarship to attend Mount Holyoke College, one of the Seven Sister schools, in Massachusetts. As a seventeen-year old, I became an emancipated adult, completely responsible for myself, so I could leave Arizona. The night I boarded the plane for my first flight was one of the happiest in my life. Ralph, Mom, Granny, and Mrs.

Reid saw me off. Ralph cried. That's when I realized that, despite our sibling battles over the years, he loved me.

Chapter 21

CAN I COME BACK

The month of May arrived as my daffodils bloomed. The pretty yellow flowers with their faint aroma accented my flower bed. As the end of my single parenthood approached, I sent out invitations to a bon voyage party for Nephew. Several people responded immediately, and I prepared for a sizable turnout.

As the days in May came and went, I had low energy. *Cinco de Mayo*, the Mexican holiday commemorating Mexico's defeat of the French in an 1862 battle, arrived, and I did nothing. At Granny's house, we celebrated the holiday faithfully. I felt stressed because my two books were spinning off competing deadlines and I had permitted myself to be roped further into university politics. I realized something, most likely my weekly newspaper column, was going to bite the dust. I couldn't foresee how I was going to continue to write it while co-authoring two books and attending all the university meetings after returning to full-time teaching.

Mother's Day descended, and Nephew mailed cards and gifts to his mom and stepmom. To me, he said nothing. My friend Orese sent me a card. I appreciated that she thought of me in this capacity.

Nephew's father called that afternoon. We typically heard a couple of times a month from my brother. He wanted to speak to his son to thank him for the gift to his wife. I called Nephew and they conversed. After the conversation ended, I noticed Nephew seemed upset.

"What's wrong?" I asked.

"I told my dad I was on punishment until I get my grades up. He told me that when I come back out there, I won't have to worry about grades."

"Ugh, that's not good."

"Auntie, he doesn't care about me," Nephew said, crying.

"He cares, sweetheart. He just doesn't always know how to show it."

Nephew continued to cry, and I put my arm around him. I wanted to throttle my brother, but I knew it wouldn't do any good to call back. He'd just get defensive. I also had to accept that when he was Nephew's age, his father Alex didn't care much about his grades. Terrance told me that Alex stayed drunk for the first three years after taking them to Long Beach. When he finally took a job, it was driving a tour bus, so he was gone for days at a time, leaving my nine-year-old half-brother in charge of the household. Terrance said his father told him he only needed to get C's so he could join the military after he graduated from high school. Mom would have never told him that. If I brought home an A minus, she thought I was slipping.

There was nothing I could do to change the fate of what happened to my half-siblings. For now, my goal was to help Nephew follow a better path, even if he perceived me as being mean and overly strict.

Outside, the wind blew something fierce as the day approached for Nephew's going-away party. Inside my home, the heat stifled the air. The smallest of my two swamp coolers quit functioning, and the bigger one didn't seem to be up for the task of cooling down the entire house by itself. I stayed up late into the night cooking for Nephew's party. The food tasted great. One dish turned out so well I wanted to save it for myself. That was a good sign that I was cooking from a place of love.

I remembered once hosting a dinner party for a friend in San Francisco. By the day of the party, I had become angry with her, and was thinking about her while making dessert. The banana cake fell. That was the first time that had ever happened to me. I inverted the two halves and placed whip cream and fresh bananas in the middle so no one could tell there was an indentation in the center. Ultimately, the cake looked and tasted delicious. Fortunately, there were other guests. One reported that he left a law firm dinner after he went outside for a breather between the main course and dessert, he then struck up a conversation with a homeless guy. He decided the homeless guy was more interesting than the lawyers and didn't return. I laughed and applauded him as I thought of all the times that I wanted to ditch a "professional" event because I was bored.

Wednesday arrived and at 3:30 p.m. Nephew brought home a posse of eight kids, including Michelle and another former girlfriend. Yesterday, he told me only two kids were coming home with him after school. When I told him the party didn't start until 5:30, he agreed to take them to the park, but not before giving them a tour of the house, including my office and bedroom. This annoyed me, but I kept my vow to stay calm and not scream at him about anything.

At 5:00 p.m., I heard the garage door open and thought Nephew had returned early. I opened the door to the garage and saw Nephew's friend Kevin putting in the code, with another kid standing by watching.

"What are you doing?" I asked Kevin.

"Opening the garage door," he replied.

"You know the code?"

"Yeah, Terrance showed me how to do it."

"Oh." I started to wonder how many kids at Jefferson Middle School had the code to get into my home.

Nephew returned with his entourage in tow. I dared not look at him because I was livid that he had showed Kevin how to get into the house.

The doorbell rang, and more guests arrived. His French teacher Mrs. Dupré and Language Arts teacher Mr. Reynolds stopped by, as did several of my friends.

Lisa gave Nephew twenty dollars as a going-away present. Mrs. Dupré and my friend Robyn brought him the last two *Lemony Snicket's A Series of Unfortunate Events* books. Throughout the year, Nephew read all of the series but these two. He had become a voracious reader. Of course, part of the reason he read so much was that he kept losing his other privileges.

The kids took to the back porch and the adults stayed inside. I split the food between the two venues. Out on the porch were Florella, Nephew's first New Mexico girlfriend, and Anita, the Amazonian-like daughter of my friend. Nephew had dated one and made a play for the other. I wanted to stay just to watch the dynamics as Nephew seemed to be living a scene from the Willy Nelson and Julio Iglesias' song "To All the Girls I've Loved Before." Moredus pointed to Florella and told Nephew, "Yeah, she's beautiful like you said."

Nephew nodded, satisfied as if he had won the prize for the having had the most beautiful girlfriend in seventh grade.

He looked at me, surrounded by his friends for support, and asked, "So, when am I going to get my bike back?"

"When you learn that a strapped helmet and a bike go together," I said.

At that moment the phone rang, and I left to go inside, but not before Nephew said, "See, I told you she was mean."

"Yep, she's mean, all right," one of his friends said in agreement. "You win."

Apparently, Nephew also won the prize for having the meanest parent in seventh grade.

Inside, I picked up the phone. "Hello."

"Hi. I need to know how to get to your house to drop off Antonio's clothes," the caller said.

"What? Who is this? What are you talking about?"

"Is this where Terrance lives?

"Ah, yeah."

"He invited my son Antonio to spend the night."

"He did *what*?"

"Terrance invited Antonio for a sleepover. He said several boys are spending the night after the party. I just need directions so I can drop off my son's clothes."

"I'm sorry, but this is the first I'm hearing about this. I never told Terrance he could have a sleepover tonight. You're welcome to drop off Antonio for the party, but he can't spend the night."

"Okay."

I gave her directions and hung up. At that very second, another kid's mother called about dropping off her son's clothes. I looked toward the back porch, but I didn't dare go out there. I took several deep breaths and steadied myself. Nephew had some nerve. He gave out the code to the garage, brought an entourage home from school, and invited kids to spend the night without asking me. No matter what happens, I vowed, "I will not scream.... I will not scream... I will not scream...."

Around six o'clock, I announced it was time for the kids to come in so Nephew could say his goodbyes and I could express a few moments of gratitude. I thanked Mr. Reynolds for giving Nephew a paper a week to write and assigning him several books to read. "You made a difference," I said. I also expressed appreciation to Mrs. Dupré for exposing Nephew to a new language. He thanked his teachers, and Lisa, Robyn, and Mrs. Dupré for their gifts. He talked about how much he liked the people he met in New Mexico, including our "weird" neighbors.

After the guests left, I called my mother on the verge of tears. "When I give an inch, he takes a mile," I said. "I told him he could bring home two kids and he brought home eight. Eight! And to top it off, he told two of them they could sleep over. I didn't find out until their mothers called about dropping off their clothes."

"Honey, it'll all be over in two days."

"Mom," I continued, ignoring her attempts to soothe my frayed nerves, "That knucklehead gave kids a tour of my office after I closed the door. I've finally got the books organized upstairs. How dare he?"

"He probably just wanted to show off where he lives. He wasn't thinking about how you might feel."

"That's it, Mom. He never thinks. How could he compromise our safety by giving out the code to the garage?"

"He probably wasn't thinking of it that way. He just wanted to share with his friends," Mom said.

"Mom, do you know how many near misses that boy has had on a bike, and he still won't wear a proper bike helmet. What's wrong with him?"

"Honey, boys are like that. They think they're invincible. Don't think about him anymore. Just make yourself some hot tea and take a hot bath. Calm yourself down."

"Good idea. Thanks for listening, Mom."

The next day, Nephew came home from school and immediately asked, "My friends want to know why I have to leave the minute school is out? I get out of school, and two hours later I'm on a plane to L.A. Bam! Just like that. I'm gone."

"I'm leaving for Wyoming on Saturday. We talked about this when we discussed having your Mom buy the ticket."

"Well, it doesn't seem fair."

"You can't stay here by yourself. It's against the law. Remember we saw on the news how those parents left their sixteen-year-old daughter in charge while they went on vacation. The police arrested them when they got home."

"I could have stayed a few more days with Kevin."

"You should have thought about that before your mom bought the ticket. You're stuck now," I said, thinking *he's getting on that plane tomorrow no matter what*. Part of me understood why he didn't want to go home so quickly, but I was too exhausted to even begin to think how to arrange for him to stay later.

"Well, it just doesn't seem fair," he repeated and marched up to his room.

When dinner was ready, I called him down. "Since this is going to be your last dinner, I cooked your favorite shrimp dish," I said.

He barely acknowledged my words and picked at his food. "Can I come back?"

"What?" I said, thinking I couldn't be hearing right.

"Can I come back? You know, for school next year."

"Why would you want to do that?" I said, still not believing my ears.

"I like Jefferson and my friends here. If I go back to Long Beach, I will be going to my third middle school in three years. I want to come back for eighth grade and graduate from Jefferson."

"But," I said, "You'd have to live here, with your mean Auntie. Surely you wouldn't want to go through that again?"

"I like living here. I know you're mean because you care about me."

"Just think, if you go back to Long Beach, you won't have to do any chores."

"That's okay. I like doing chores."

"Yeah, but there won't be anybody putting you on punishment for not doing your homework."

"That's okay," he said, beginning to cry.

"There won't be anyone to take away your sports and girl privileges when you get bad grades. You'll be able to do whatever you want."

Nephew cried openly, and my heart melted. I took the chair closest to him and pulled him to my shoulder. "It's okay, sweetheart. I tell you what."

His ears perked up.

"You have been working hard. If you make at least a 3.0 on your final semester report card, we'll talk about you coming back."

"Okay, Auntie," he said and started to pull himself together.

As I cleaned up, I still felt shocked by what had just transpired. I thought the boy would be as happy to go as I was to have him leave. This living together had been exhausting for both of us.

Friday dawned. Nephew's last day. He placed his suitcases in the Saab before walking to school. I offered him a ride, but he said he wanted to walk one last time. I felt his sadness.

Around 3:30 p.m., I picked him up at Jefferson to take him to the airport. At the Southwest Airlines ticket counter, the agent asked if I would like to go back to the gate with him. Although he was now thirteen and could walk to the gate by himself, I elected to walk with him.

After we passed security, I felt myself begin to cry. At the gate, I gave Nephew a hug. "Thank you, sweetheart."

"For what, Auntie?"

"For teaching me how to be a parent."

"You're welcome, Auntie." His eyes began to mist.

"See you soon, sweetheart," I said, waving goodbye.

When I returned home, I noticed the package my friend Cecilia had sent earlier in the week. On the phone, she told me to open it at the party, but I forgot. I retrieved the scissors and cut off the brown wrapping paper. Inside, I found a gold-plated statute of a woman with wings holding up her hands in triumph with a torch in her right hand. The caption read:

Sherri Burr
Aunt of the Year

I laughed.

Three weeks later, I received Nephew's final report card in the mail. He earned six B's and one A, a 3.14 GPA, the highest of the year. Last year, he finished sixth grade by receiving every grade on the scale, including a D and F. This year, he ended seventh grade with nothing lower than a B. Further, he was no longer fat. He walked onto the airplane two inches taller and

20 pounds trimmer than when he arrived. And, it seemed he was still a virgin. I called Nephew to invite him back to attend eighth grade. He excitedly accepted.

* * *

I was glad the connection gap with Nephew would be far less than the time between my half siblings being kidnapped and when we saw them again. Between the two of us, Ralph was the first to reconnect. While I was out of the country interning at the Agency for International Development in Dar es Salam, Tanzania, he wrote me.

"Guess what?" he penned in his letter delivered through the diplomatic pouch, "Terrance, Butch and Joyce were in Phoenix during the fourth of July holidays. It was really a sensation to see them. I must admit they sure did look beautiful. Sherri you wouldn't believe how Joyce made me feel as I observed her for the first time in a long time. She sure is a bright young girl. She also is the splitting image of you. She possesses all the characteristics that you possess. Furthermore, what makes me so proud is the feeling I get in knowing that both of you are my sisters." This was during the days when Vera went by a shortened version of her middle name.

His letter continued, "As for Terrance and Butch, I feel they are both intelligent in their own ways. You know Sherri it is strange how our heavenly Creator sets forth a path for each person born into the world he created. If a person selects to journey the path given to him by our creator then his journey will be successful.

But if a person selects to travel a different journey than the one given by our creator, then that person will find his journey very unpleasant. I feel this same issue applies to Terrance and Butch, very much so because if they chose to travel the correct path then their journey will be beautiful, but on the same token if they do not, then it will be up to me to guide then. I can tell Joyce already knows her path."

Ralph's letter turned out to be prophetic in more ways than one. His words about choosing the right path would also refer to Nephew, our half-brother Terrance's first-born son.

Chapter 23

THAT DOCTOR'S A TOTAL LOSER

When I looked at Nephew across the dinner table during his seventh-grade year, I often thought of my siblings. His natural charm with women reminded me of his father, Terrance Senior, who was also a beautiful baby. His natural athleticism recalled moments of watching my brothers Butch and Ralph play sports. When Nephew's face occasionally filled with sadness, I was reminded of the forlorn expression on my half-sister Vera's visage when I met her again following ten years of forced separation. I could never completely feel her pain from having been wrenched from Mom's and my care when she was age two. I knew only what it felt like to have had her snatched.

Despite the challenges, I felt blessed to continue my relationship with my half-brother's son. I spent time with him that I missed spending with my half-siblings when they were his age.

Nephew returned to spend eighth grade at Jefferson. As a companion in my home, he was a joy. I resumed full-time teaching at the University of New Mexico and published my first two books. With numerous deadlines, I would often call home and ask

Nephew to prepare dinner. He also sometimes did my share of the housework, and I doubled his allowance.

I occasionally invited folks over to dinner to broaden his horizons of potential career options. Since he had once expressed an interest in becoming a doctor, I invited over an anesthesiologist who I had met at a table-for-six type dinner to connect single people. While, I wasn't attracted to him, I did think Nephew might enjoy hearing about his take on the medical profession.

Unfortunately, the Asian doctor, who stood about five-foot, seven-inches tall on a slender frame, started complaining during dinner about how he couldn't get women to date him. He slipped into the conversation that he made $250,000 a year.

After he left, Nephew declared, "That doctor's a total looser."

"What? He makes $250,000 a year," I responded.

"Well, if I made $250,000 a year, I would go to the club and announce to all the girls, Look at me. I'm the $250k, man. Yeah, that's right, I make $250,000 a year. The girls would swarm," he said, confidently.

"When you look like you and have your charm, you don't need to make $250,000 a year. The girls naturally flock to you."

"Yeah, and if I looked like that doctor, I could still get girls if they knew I made $250,000 a year. That doctor doesn't know anything about women."

I just raised my hands and let him have the last word.

Nephew saved his money to purchase a bike. Unlike with the one his mother sent the money for him to purchase or the one his friend gave him during Jefferson Pride night in seventh grade, Nephew never lost his bike privileges. He still owns that bike.

He made better grades during eighth grade and rarely lost any privileges. Indeed, on his first progress report, he earned four A's and two B's, a 3.6 GPA. His grades never dropped below a 3.0.

As eighth grade ended, our family debated whether he should remain in New Mexico for high school or depart for Long Beach. His mother and father, along with Mom and my brother Ralph, urged him to remain in New Mexico since he seemed to be doing so well. I told him he was welcome to stay. We checked out Albuquerque High School and the Amy Biehl Charter School, while he expressed interest in Sandia High School where several of his Jefferson friends were going.

Nephew decided to return to Long Beach. He said, "If I stay any longer, I would have spent half my schooling in New Mexico. My mom will no longer be my mom. You will be."

I honored his decision.

***

While our immediate family might have felt it best for Nephew to stay in New Mexico, I remained haunted when Alex refused to accept that Mom's kids should stay with her. Almost a decade passed before I eventually re-encountered Nephew's father and our other half-siblings after the kidnapping. I was twenty-two and had just finished my first year at Yale Law School. By then, Terrance was sixteen, Butch fifteen, and Vera twelve. Butch and Vera did not remember me. Butch had long since forgotten our expeditions into the foothills of South Mountain to hunt jack rabbits. Vera had no recollection that she used to call me "My Sherri" because I took care of her. Only Terrance vaguely remembered me. It was as if Alex stole their memories when he kidnapped them.

In my academic research, I later read about how many kidnappers endeavor to alienate their captives from potential rescuers so they will accept the situation. What happened to my siblings inspired me to write a law review article about the illegality of kidnapping under international law.

Chapter 24

I DIDN'T THINK SHE WAS OVULATING

Friends who met Nephew during his years of visiting New Mexico often asked me, "How is Nephew? What is he doing now?"

During his freshman year back in Long Beach, I became alarmed when Nephew reported that his Mom had placed him on punishment for a month for violating her rules, but he didn't have to serve it because his cousins were visiting. One lesson I learned from parenting him was the importance of consistency. After the first bike episode, I realized I should never state a punishment that I was not prepared to carry out. On the phone, he gave the impression he could do whatever he wanted. I stressed that was not necessarily good for him or his mother. Mary seemed to feel criticized when I hinted that she should enforce whatever punishment she imposed. Imposing a day of restrictions was better than imposing a month of restrictions if he only served a day. With such limited guidance, Nephew seemed to be jumping out of planes without parachutes.

While visiting Albuquerque during the summer following his freshman year, he told me he had started having sex with his girlfriend. Realizing the proverbial cat was out of the bag, I took him to Target, and we walked down the birth control aisle. I recommended he use two methods to increase his chance of preventing pregnancy. He expressed embarrassment, so I recommended he immediately stop having sex before it was too late. When he had me talk to his girlfriend by phone, I told her, "Quit having sex with my nephew."

She broke up with Nephew, and he got mad at me. But they got back together.

Several months later, I received a call from my sister, Vera, who said Nephew had impregnated his girlfriend. She was angry with Mary, Nephew's mother, for not supervising him more closely.

Knowing Nephew as I did, I realized only one person was responsible. When I followed-up, Nephew said, "I didn't think she was ovulating."

"How would you know that? Were you charting the temperatures of her cycle?" I asked.

"No, I just didn't think...."

"Isn't that often the problem, Nephew, you don't think before you act."

After we hung up, I booked a Southwest Airlines flight to California. I wanted to meet the young lady and her family. In their living room, I cried and apologized for my nephew's actions toward their daughter. That didn't sit well with Nephew and his mother. Indeed, the girl was older than Nephew. Perhaps her family should have been apologizing to us.

Nephew's child was born to fanfare as my brother and his mother Mary embraced the idea of becoming grandparents. When they told me of his daughter's birth who they reported looked just like him, I cried for an hour. Tears flowed down my face and drenched the pillow. I was concerned that Nephew would become the kind of teenage father who never finished high school, let alone went to college, and ended up working dead-end jobs.

As the end of his high school years approached, Nephew was earning two A's and four F's. Mom and I visited him in Long Beach while Mary planned a prom party for Nephew. I was scratching my head, wondering why he wasn't studying. I would have banned prom until I received assurances that he had the grades to finish. Like with the birth of his daughter, I felt I was in some time warp. Mary didn't seem to see what I saw. To not graduate from high school would negatively affect his entire life.

Finally, I told Nephew that if he graduated, I would give him either the Saab or a thousand dollars. Nephew scraped through with two grades of A and four grades of D-. He chose the cash, and express-mailed his report card and diploma so I could pay up. His final high school transcript contained about 40% A's, 40% F's, with a smattering of B's and C's. When I asked him about it, he admitted that if he liked the teacher and the subject, he did the work. If not, he did nothing.

Chapter 25

YOU'RE SENDING ME BACK TO JOBLESSNESS AND HOMELESSNESS

Nephew enrolled and dropped out of college three times. He even considered Central New Mexico College (CNM) in Albuquerque and actually started classes. After noticing him goofing off while his buddy Kevin worked and studied, I finally gave up. I told Nephew if he returned to Long Beach, I would pay his tuition and his apartment fees if he found a roommate.

He became very angry and proclaimed, "You're sending me back to joblessness and homelessness."

Nephew returned to Long Beach. Instead of going to college, however, he moved in with his new girlfriend and found jobs as a security guard and a bus driver. They married on *Cinco de Mayo* 2012 when Nephew was 22. At his wedding reception, Nephew told his guests about my influence on his life. Tears emerged, as I felt the sacrifices were worthwhile.

I offered to use frequent flier miles to send them on a honeymoon trip to either Europe or Hawaii as their wedding gift. Nephew chose Europe. The tickets I found took them from L.A. to Rome and from Paris to L.A. Nephew finally made it to Paris.

During the year before Nephew's marriage, my father and stepfather, John and Alex, died in their seventies within four months of each other. John fell off a ladder while painting his home and cracked his skull. He lingered in a coma for a few days before passing. While he had prepaid many of his funeral expenses, he had not covered the grave opening and closing, which cost about $1500. His wife Annie asked me to pay. I thought it ironic that I provided funds to bury a father who rarely supported me during my childhood.

Spending time at John's home after his death I saw his bedroom for the first time in decades. I noticed the purple accent walls and wondered how it was possible that Ralph and I had independently painted purple accent walls in our homes. Could this desire for purple be a genetic trait? John had often commented that although I looked like my mother, I had his ways. I didn't believe him until he drove my standard-shift Honda Civic like a go-cart. I became so notorious for driving the car as fast as possible down San Francisco's crooked Lombard Street while I worked for a law firm that my colleagues joked if they ever needed a getaway driver, they would hire me. John also had a strong entrepreneurial streak and a penchant for purchasing real estate. Those traits, which I seemed to also have inherited, I would later track back through his family for centuries.

John's funeral at his local church was packed and he was extolled as a great man who often helped others. That day, I sat next to my brother Ralph's two children as I learned more about my father from those who knew him best during his later years. Eventually, I accepted that a part of him was part of me.

Alex, Nephew's grandfather, passed away from kidney failure at the end of June 2011. My half-brother Terrance reported Alex stopped dialysis so he could die. My half-sister Vera lived with Alex until his final trip to the hospital. Terrance said the only way Alex escaped being responsible for his youngest children was through death. By kidnapping them, Alex had created his own prison in which he served a life sentence.

In addition to being a kidnapper, Alex had been a victim of kidnapping. Terrance said Alex's first wife had left with her daughter and their three kids while he was at work. Alex came home from work one day to a completely cleaned-out house. No family, no furniture, nothing.

Mom, unfortunately, did not know that Alex had been married before and what had happened to him. Such trauma meant that Mom unwittingly married a ticking time bomb. It was only a matter of time before Alex exploded and devastated our lives.

Terrance thought his father may have started a third family during his long-haul bus trips. Alex once brought home a baby who looked like him. Terrance recalled watching Alex bathe the baby and lotion his body and butt. The retelling of Alex placing lotion on the baby's rear end sent chills down my spine. Terrance said he never saw the baby again.

With some trepidation, I went to California soon after Alex died to offer emotional support to my half-siblings. I took Ralph's children with me so they could experience Disneyland. We did not stay for the funeral after Vera decided to set it for ten days later so their relatives could fly in from all over the country. Vera began searching for their first set of half siblings and found that one of them was a former cop who was in jail for child abuse.

As Vera and Terrance finalized arrangements for Alex's services and internment at a military cemetery because he had been a veteran of the Korean War, Butch asked to borrow $1000 to upgrade Alex's casket while he lay in cold storage at the funeral home. The difference between the $1595 casket and the $2595 casket was that the latter had more steel and moveable handles.

My blood pressure rose as I contemplated the request. I had worked with a therapist to find the courage to forgive Alex and myself. Because I had helped pack my half-sibling's bags for the "vacation" Alex said he was taking them on, I blamed myself for being deceived. The therapist said Alex probably would have killed Mom if he hadn't stolen her children, considering how he was escalating the violence against her.

I kept my money and suggested Butch and Vera stick to the budget set by Alex's insurance policy.

Butch raged about burying Alex in "a cheap-ass casket." At the funeral, Butch told Nephew, "We're not speaking to your Auntie."

Nephew reported that fifteen people attended Alex's services. No children from his first marriage participated.

When I looked back on the seven years we lived with Alex, I couldn't recall a single friend of his that we ever met besides his family members. Mom didn't shed a single tear after either of her former husbands died.

A couple of years after Alex passed away, I read Rachel Louise Snyder's *No Visible Bruises: What We don't Know About Domestic Violence Can Kill Us* (New York: Bloomsbury Publishing, 2019) and finally understood what Granny had known that fateful night. Our situation with Mom's second husband reeked of danger. If Granny had not stood up to Alex, then Mom, and maybe all of us, might have ended up dead. Snyder's book discussed the Domestic Violence Danger Assessment, which asked the following questions that I answered.

(1) *Has he strangled you?* Ralph and I witnessed Alex grab Mom by the neck in the car on the trip to Morenci to visit his parents.

(2) *Beaten you while pregnant?* A beating that we did not witness may have preceded Mom losing Tony Jeffrey, her fourth child with Alex. She was most

likely pregnant with Terrance, her first child with Alex, when we were on our way to Morenci, Arizona, to meet his family. When we arrived, he beat Mom in front of her family as they watched. Not a single person intervened.

(3) *Does he have access to a gun?* I didn't recall seeing a gun in our home, but Alex could shoot because he had served in the Korean War.

(4) *Is he a substance abuser?* Alex was a raging alcoholic.

(5) *Is he unemployed or underemployed?* When we first moved in with Alex, he was employed with the Coca-Cola Bottling Company as a driver. But he must have lost his job around the time Mom miscarried because he was around the house in the daytime.

(6) *Are there children in the home that aren't his?* Yes: Ralph and me.

(7) *Has he threatened to kill you?* While I never heard Alex issue a threat that severe, I was not always with Alex when he was with Mom.

(8) *Threatened to kill himself?* I never heard him issue suicide-type words.

(9) *Threatened to hurt the children?* On the fateful night, I heard him say to Mom that if she didn't have sex with him, "I'm going to go get Sherri." I perceived those words as a threat against my pre-teen body. Also, Alex didn't just whip Ralph if he did something wrong, he *beat* him with a belt, using violence beyond corrective action.

(10) *Has he ever avoided being arrested for domestic violence?* No one ever called the cops on Alex. I called Granny and she took care of the situation. ...

Our family situation with my stepfather scored high on this danger assessment. Among the other points that Snyder made was: "As dangerous as it is in the home, it is almost more dangerous to leave." Mom was protected while we lived with Granny because, not only did she have a gun, so did Grandpa and Mom's brother, who also lived in their home. Alex may have known this because he stopped engaging in any direct confrontations with Mom.

Snyder also said that the leading cause of death for young African American women is homicide. If not for Granny standing up to Alex, Mom might have become a statistic when she was 32 years of age. Snyder added that the "single biggest risk for domestic homicide ... is the prior incidence of domestic violence. ... Dangerousness spiked when the victim attempted to leave an abuser, and it stayed very high for three months, then dipped only slightly for the next nine months. After a year, the dangerousness dropped off precipitously."

After leaving Alex, Mom remained at high risk for homicide. It was during this period that, instead of killing Mom, he stole her kids. I have no doubt that he deceived us to mask his true intentions because Granny had put the fear of God in him.

No wonder Mom shed no tears when Alex died. And I definitely decided not to contribute to his funeral.

Mom never spoke an ill word about Alex or John during their lifetimes and continued her silence after their deaths. Ralph and I were left to form our own opinions of the men she married. The only time we protested was when she wanted to marry a third time to a tall, handsome, dark-skinned man. After our gambling father had left us and our alcoholic stepfather had kidnapped our half-siblings, we were afraid of Mom's husband-picking genes. We told her if she got married again, we were not going to live with her and planned to stay with Granny. Mom broke off her engagement.

Five years before Nephew moved in to start seventh grade, Granny passed away at the age of eighty-five in 1997. Her services were attended by Nephew and over two hundred people, but not by my half-siblings Terrance, Butch and Vera. Aunt Liz said their absence was my stepfather Alex's final act of revenge. In my eulogy, I recounted how Granny stood up to Alex and demonstrated women did not have to be victims. The 100th anniversary of Granny's birth coincided with Easter Sunday in 2012, the year of Nephew's first marriage. To commemorate the occasion, my cousin Derrick and I met at her gravesite and thanked her for her presence in our lives. To this day, Granny remains the person I most admire.

My brother Ralph passed away in 2017, five years after Derrick and I celebrated Granny's birth anniversary. Ralph had suffered a heart attack in

November 2008, lost oxygen to the brain for over 22 minutes, and remained in a semi-vegetative state as I became his guardian for the rest of his life. Nephew flew over to provide words at his funeral in Phoenix. He recalled how Ralph had provided comfort in Las Vegas to help him recover from the basketball incident.

Chapter 26

SHE DIDN'T KNOW

Mom was living in Albuquerque at the time both of her former husbands died. Initially, she was just supposed to move to New Mexico for six months in 2007, but then she liked it. Mom moved to Victorville, California, in 2012 to spend more time with my half-brother and Nephew's father, Terrance Senior. In her own way, Mom wanted to make amends for Alex's actions that separated her from her children. I supported the venture by paying most of her rent and visiting quarterly.

For two years, Mom lived closer to Nephew than I did. She frequently saw him and his family. Then one night in November 2014, I received a call from her. "Get me out of here," she said firmly. Because Mom normally spoke softly with a southern tinge to her voice, this command was out of character and felt urgent. Throughout my life, Mom had occasionally reminded me that she gave me life. "I shed my blood for you," she said.

Those words reduced me to silence, and I did her bidding.

Within a week, I flew to Victorville, rented a moving truck and drove her back to Albuquerque to settle her into a fourth-floor apartment overlooking a castle-like home.

Nephew stayed married for several years. His wife gave birth to their son. Eventually, they divorced.

Nephew had additional children within new relationships. He brought both his second son and second daughter and their mothers to visit me in New Mexico over the course of three years. After he arrived with his second daughter, we stopped by my friend Orese's home. Orese and Nephew's two-year old walked hand in hand as he and I sat down at a round cast-iron outdoor table on a crisp spring New Mexico day with the sun shining bright above us as clouds moved sporadically above. Once his child had been led out of earshot, Nephew leaned in and told me for the first time that he had been sexually abused by his babysitter between the ages of five and eight.

I felt tears well up as I listened to him recount how the babysitter who was five years older than him had forced him to have intercourse. Since he had not gone through puberty, this activity caused his testicles to swell. "Didn't you have hernia surgeries? That's what your mother told me," I said.

"No," he said emphatically. "The surgeries were to release the build-up in my testicles that were causing tremendous pain."

"But your mother …."

"She didn't know. The babysitter was the daughter of a friend of hers. And I fell in love with the babysitter."

"But you were a child," I protested. The lawyer part of my soul wanted to reach back in time and have the babysitter arrested for child abuse. At the same time, it occurred to me that she had probably been abused herself to be so sexually active at such an early age.

"The abuse stopped when I changed schools, and I no longer went there after school," Nephew said.

"Oh my God," I asked, "is this why you told me you had a girlfriend when you were in second grade and came to Hawaii? You said that you liked older women."

"Yep," Nephew confirmed.

My heart grieved for his lost innocence. I thought about his expressed desire to go to school in Hawaii. If only I had known that he was being abused. I would have done my darndest to set up my life so he could attend school in Honolulu. Nephew's revelation also brought a new perspective on what might have caused all those girls to gravitate towards him. When he was twelve, I thought it was his handsomeness, incredible charm, and the pheromones he put out once he entered puberty. My poor nephew. I had been called to manage a situation that had additional layers of complexity when he moved into my Albuquerque home.

We both cried and hugged each other.

Chapter 27

I CAN CATCH THE NEXT PLANE

There are no treatments left," the cardiologist said on August 2, 2024, as he looked as scans of Mom's legs showing blood clots. "With her brain surgery two weeks ago, we can't give her Xarelto to thin out the clots because that medicine may have caused her brain bleed."

"What are Mom's options?" I asked as tears welled up in my eyes. Mom's dual problems of congestive heart failure and kidney failure had coalesced. After surgery involving drilling a Burr Hole with the diameter of a straw to relieve a spontaneous brain bleed, she improved in the Neuro ICU and on the neuro floor of the hospital. Less than a week after the surgery, Mom had been sent to rehab. Their treatments of administering the drug Lasik to address the swelling in her legs and had caused Mom to deteriorate and the rehab center returned her to the hospital.

The cardiologist continued speaking as he looked from Mom to me and back again. "Mrs. Peete, do you want to be placed on home hospice where you can receive comfort care or be sent to the ICU? Because you are full code, if you stop breathing, we will be required to do everything possible to bring you back when you stop breathing. Not sure you would want that because those treatments can break ribs, causing more pain, and ultimately be unsuccessful."

"How long?" I asked when Mom didn't respond.

"About two weeks," he said.

I went to the bathroom and started wailing. After I somewhat calmed myself, I returned to Mom and asked, "What do you want to do? The choice is yours."

"Call your brother," she said. "See if he can come out and help you."

"If Terrance Senior is not available, can I also call Terrance Junior?" I asked, knowing that my brother had a lot of medical issues of his own whereas my nephew was currently unemployed after injuring his back while working as a bus driver.

Mom promptly nodded her head. I called my brother Terrance, Mom's third child and her oldest son remaining after my brother Ralph died from heart disease seven years before. I explained the situation to Terrance. "Mom should definitely do hospice," he said. "She should go live with you."

"When can you come out?" I asked.

"Let me talk to my wife. Tomorrow, we have the goodbye party for my granddaughter who's going away to college in Alabama. I can probably come the day after that."

After we hung up, I called Terrance Junior, the oldest of Mom's grandchildren who I continued to call just "Nephew."

"Tomorrow's my daughter's graduation party but I can catch the next plane," he said. I told him I would be using Southwest Airlines points to book flights for both him and his father.

True to his word, Nephew arrived the next day. He wanted to immediately see his grandmother. Mom's face lit up when he walked into the room.

As I looked at her smooth face, I found it hard to believe that Mom could be about to exit stage left of life. When the hospitalist came in and said he was placing an order for home hospice, I challenged him and said we would prefer home health. I mentioned Harmony Home Health and Hospice, which had restored Mom after several hospital visits.

He pushed back and said he could only release Mom to hospice. I asked for a second opinion.

The hospitalist who had taken care of Mom two weeks before when she was on the neuro floor came up. He was from Sudan, and Mom and I came to immediately appreciate his calm presence and helpfulness at that time. After debating the pros and cons of hospice versus home health, we settled on hospice because Harmony said they had patients who had graduated from hospice to home health. Deep within me, I wanted to believe that Mom could recover with the same home medical team that had restored her health before. I had to have hope.

A flurry of activity commenced as Harmony sent a hospital bed, and I had to figure out where it could go. The main floor of my house had two bedrooms and a bathroom that had been handicap retrofitted to accommodate Mom's previous recovery stays at my home. My friend Jim, who Mom had verbally adopted and introduced to nursing staff as her son, came over. We tried to remove the bed in Mom's favorite room with a view over the city of Albuquerque. When we couldn't undue what Jim had previously done to stabilize the bed without destroying the frame, we opted to put Mom's hospice bed in the room that I used as my office by removing most of the furniture. We moved the twin bed from the office to the dining room.

That settled, I returned to the hospital. Mom was loaded into an ambulance for transport to my home and I drove Nephew. I offered him the choice of sleeping in Mom's regular bedroom, on the twin bed in the dining room, or downstairs in the remodeled lower-level basement apartment. Nephew chose Mom's regular room to be close to her.

The next day, I picked up my brother from the airport. He chose to quarter downstairs.

On August 6th, we all convened in Mom's room. The right side of her head still contained the stitches from the brain surgery, which were due to be removed in two weeks. After we greeted Mom, my brother asked if she knew what day it was.

"It's August 6th, Terrance's birthday," Mom promptly replied, proving the brain surgery had not affected her memory regarding her second-born son. My brother's face lit up with delight.

I baked a moist banana chocolate chip cake with chocolate frosting to serve after supper. We sang "Happy Birthday, Terrance" as he blew out the candles. I thought about his sixth birthday at Hermosa Park. How happy that occasion had been only to have tragedy strike a week later when he was kidnapped.

My brother Terrance left the next day, while Nephew stayed.

The hospice nurse trained me on how to administer Mom's comfort meds to address pain. I trained Nephew on how to take Mom's blood pressure, temperature, O2 and pulse numbers to monitor her vitals, all of which I had learned during Mom's prior post-hospital stays in my home. We set the oxygen concentrator or a portable tank full tank at two liters for Mom to receive oxygen full time. Previously, she only used one liter at night.

When Mom experienced severe constipation and cried out with discomfort, Nephew donned gloves to relieve compacted fecal matter. Upon the recommendation of Mom's doctor, we started administering Tylenol at regular intervals rather than wait until Mom was in severe pain and we had to give her morphine. I made a red lentil soup and Nephew mastered the art of crushing up pills to blend into the soup.

In between taking care of Mom, Nephew and I took turns taking breaks to walk around the neighborhood or run errands so that someone was always with her.

On Sunday, August 25th, Mom was having a great day, so Nephew interviewed her about her life. He asked if she had any advice for her children, grandchildren or great-grandchildren. "Make the day the best day you can." For me, she said, "Tell Sherri to get her hair done."

I read Mom my draft of what I called her life story, knowing that it would eventually become her obituary. Mom, who had taught me to read and do puzzles as a two-year old, approved every word. We called family members and friends so Mom could talk to them.

At the close of the day, I said to Nephew, "This feels like an ending." He agreed.

A few days later as we gathered in the kitchen after feeding Mom breakfast, Nephew said, "I have something to tell you."

We sat down on the front porch of my foothills home looking out at Albuquerque's Sandia Mountains. "What's up?" I asked.

"I had another baby," he said.

I started laughing as Nephew looked at me stunned as if he was expecting a scolding for having another child when he couldn't afford the child support for his other four kids. Indeed, the state of California had suspended his drivers license for non-payment of child support as his obligations continued after he quit his job as a bus driver.

After my laughter subsided, I said, "At this point, I expect you to produce a child a decade. I will just keep welcoming them into our family fold."

"Really?" he asked.

"Of course. You said you were going to get a vasectomy after child number three. Then after child number four. Now you have five. Only you can decide how many children you want to support."

He took out his phone to show me the picture of his newest daughter, a dumpling of a girl who was 11 months old.

"I look forward to meeting her," I said. "She looks like you. In fact, they all do."

On Saturday morning, August 31st, Mom kept looking at the clock. She refused to eat, drink, or swallow any medicines. Nephew sat with her to watch "Northern Exposure," a television series about a New York doctor who is forced to practice in rural Alaska to repay the state for covering his medical school tuition and fees. Mom, always the nurse, loved the show and nicknamed the moose in the credits, "Henry." As Mom's breathing became more labored, I slowly turned up the oxygen concentrator to provide more air and I administered small doses of morphine.

Shortly before 11:00 a.m. that Saturday, Nephew called out, "Granny wants to get out of bed."

I rushed in her room and together Nephew and I lifted Mom out of the hospital bed and into her wheelchair. She felt heavy. Before, Nephew, who weighed over 200 pounds, managed this routine of placing 160-pound Mom in her wheelchair or bathroom chair on his own. This time, I had to hold Mom's arms around him as he maneuvered her on to her chair. We attached her to portable oxygen and cranked up the number to 5 liters. I took her blood pressure and called the on-call Saturday hospice nurse after seeing weird numbers.

Nephew and I wheeled Mom to her favorite place in my living room overlooking the city. She took one look at the view and breathed out a heavy breath and slumped her head over. "Mom," I yelled. I took her vitals and got a high blood pressure (250/112), but no pulse. I called Mom's primary doctor and my neighbor who was a retired ER doctor. "Can someone have a blood pressure but no pulse," I frantically asked Mom's primary doctor.

"Try waking her up," he said.

"Let's get Mom to the porch," I told Nephew. We wheeled her to the porch, and I took another round of vitals. No blood pressure and no pulse. I yelled, "MOM, COME BACK. COME BACK!'

Nephew and I hugged her. I called the hospice nurse, Mom's doctor, our friend Jim and Reverend Charles Becknell, Jr.

The on-call hospice nurse, Jim, and Mom's primary care doctor arrived quickly. I left a message for Rev. Charles. The nurse listened to Mom's chest for 60 seconds per protocol. She looked at me and shook her head. She asked what arrangements I wanted for Mom.

I told her I had started pre-planning with French's mortuary. The hospice nurse called French's. While they were on the phone, she asked me when I wanted them to pick up Mom. "You can have up to 24 hours," she said.

I looked at Nephew. "Two hours?"

He nodded.

"Let's pray for Mom," I said. We all gathered around and held hands as Nephew, who had been training to be a minister, prayed for Mom's safe passage on her next journey.

I said to the hospice nurse and doctor, "We need to call Aunt Liz while you are here."

When I reached Aunt Liz, who had flown out to see Mom two weeks before, I explained what happened. She refused to believe that her sister passed away. I asked the nurse and doctor to confirm Mom's death, which they did. Aunt Liz still protested. They stated again that her sister had died. Recognizing the futility of continuing the conversation, I told Aunt Liz that I would keep her abreast of funeral plans and said goodbye.

After the nurse and doctor left, Reverend Charles arrived with his wife and mother. We once again formed a circle around Mom. This time, Reverend Charles prayed.

French's Mortuary sent two young ladies to pick up Mom. Nephew and I showed them where she was on the porch. They brought out their gurney, and we wheeled Mom as close as possible. It took all four of us to lift Mom from her wheelchair to the gurney. Normally people die in bed, the workers explained, and they move them using sheets. I now understood the meaning of dead weight. Mom felt like she weighed several times her normal body weight.

After Mom left my home for the last time, Nephew and I started contacting people to let them know that Mom had died. With Labor Day coming up the next Monday, we wouldn't be able to make funeral arrangements until Tuesday. Fortunately, French's Mortuary planner transferred all the pre-plans to a funeral arranger. We agreed that Mom would receive an Albuquerque viewing and memorial service on Tuesday evening, September 10th and be flown to Phoenix two days later. Several months before, I had pre-planned final resting places for Mom, Aunt Liz, and myself at Resthaven Cemetery, which already contained the remains of Mom's mother, first-born son Ralph, and first husband John Lincoln Burr.

Nephew flew back to California for a few days to regroup. He returned just as my best friend from law school, Sabrina McCarthy, came to stay with us. She took up residence in the same basement apartment where my brother Terrance had stayed. Since she had been visiting Santa Fe with some of her college friends, Sabrina brought food from the house they had rented. Sabrina provided much needed comfort and proved a calm stabilizing presence.

When we arrived at the French Mortuary Chapel the night of the funeral, the funeral director met us. During the planning process, she had said the most amount of flower arrangements she had ever seen had been eleven. This evening before she pulled open the door to the chapel, she said, "Prepare yourself."

We walked in to find sixteen flower arrangements surrounding Mom as she held court in her light pink Mother's Casket. The arrangements had been sent by family and friends from all around the country. Mom was wearing the lavender pink leisure suit and color matching crocheted cap that she created herself. Nephew and I had picked out her final outfit to match the pink Mother's Casket. We also had the funeral staff put on the pink watch that Cousin Cheryl had given Mom. Pink symbolized love and we wanted Mom to know that she was surrounded by love.

Sabrina sat next to me at the memorial service, and Nephew sat next to Reverend Charles in the front.

I spoke for twenty minutes about Mom's impact on my life and how there would have not been a professor or author Sherri Burr had I not been born to her. I spoke about Mom's independent streak. She had told her minister father, who was leading Civil Rights marches in Phoenix, that she had registered as a Republican. Her father started to protest until Mom reminded him that she had joined the party of Lincoln. I spoke of Mom's nursing training and how my brother Ralph and I had been in the audience when she graduated with honors.

Nephew spoke about visiting Mom when she lived in Phoenix. He was about five when she had walked him down to the Chicken Shack. The bag containing their meal became soaked with grease, but he remembered it as the best chicken he had ever tasted. He also declared that taking care of his grandmother during her final month had changed his life. He planned to become a hospice nurse.

Nephew's speech was followed by one from her doctor who talked about how Mom had interviewed HIM before accepting him as her doctor. For two years Mom had stopped coming in for check-ups. I suggested to her doctor that he attend Mom's 75th birthday party. He did, and she then asked me to schedule an appointment to see him.

Her occupational therapist spoke about how Mom took an interest in her and colleagues. She said Mom startled her when she referred to me as "The Baby." Two of my law professor colleagues, Alfred and Nathalie, and our friend Robert spoke after. Alfred recalled asking Mom about her decision to become a Republican. She told him of her fondness for Eisenhower, the president who had sent the 101st Airborne Division and federalized the Arkansas National Guard to enforce desegregation at Little Rock's Central High School. Having just recently graduated from Yerger High School in Hope, Arkansas, at the time, Mom had followed the developments and admired Eisenhower's bravery.

Nathalie spoke in amazement of playing the game Cashflow with Mom who was quick to answer the call to loan her sister-in-law money, even when it would result in her bankruptcy. Robert expressed admiration for Mom's knowledge of Westerns, which he had watched with her while I was out of town.

The ceremony wrapped with the Albuquerque Mayor's office reading a plaque declaring September 10, 2024, as Ola Mae Burr Peete Day in Albuquerque and the New Mexico Nurses Honor Guard saluting Mom's nursing service. As they lit a candle and read the Florence Nightingale Tribute, dozens of audience members began to weep. After ringing bells, they read the last line, "Ola Mae Burr Peete, we thank you and officially release you from your nursing duties."

Two days later, Mom took her final flight to Phoenix, as Nephew and I drove. Since Mom had always liked apartments on the second or higher floors with views, I had chosen a Mausoleum to entomb her final remains. I called it Mom's final apartment in the sky. At the Phoenix ceremony, I spoke, followed by my brother Terrance, Nephew, and Cousin Cheryl. Aunt Liz did not show up, although she had asked me to keep her name in the program. This time, it was the Arizona Nurses Honor Guard that released Mom from her nursing duties.

Afterwards, Mom's pink casket was lifted on a conveyor belt assembly to her final resting place. I thought about all that she had suffered at the hands of my gambling father and alcoholic stepfather. I recalled how she had triumphed by going to nursing school and the happiness in her face when she graduated with honors. I was happy that I had brought joy into her life by moving her to Albuquerque and introducing her to my friends who became her friends. Mom's body was placed in her forever apartment, and her spirit had ascended to the warm embrace of her relatives and friends.

Nephew flew back to California to start his nursing training on Monday, and I drove to Albuquerque. I paid his tuition to get him started in this new field following in Mom's footsteps. Our paths, which had initially connected in Phoenix when he was 11 months old at my grandmother's home, had reconvened thirty-four years later in the same city so we could say final goodbyes to our ancestor whom we both loved.

Mom with toddler Sherri in Phoenix's South Mountain

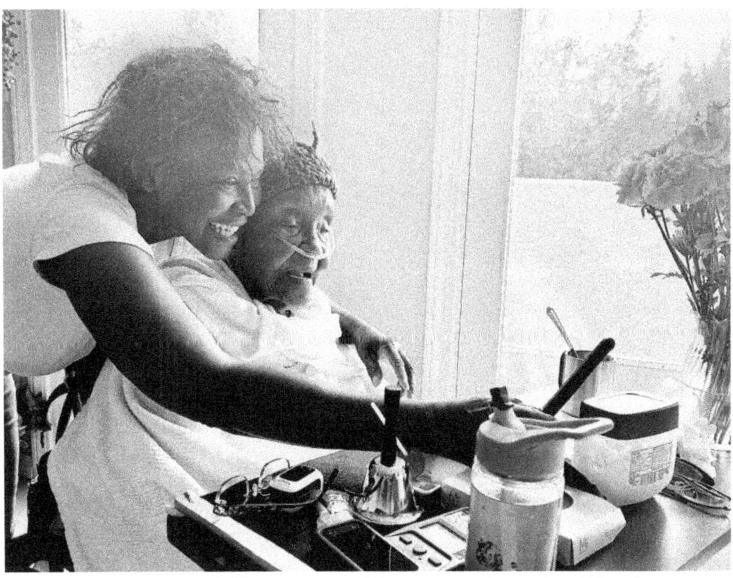

Last photo of Sherri and Mom, taken by Nephew

Terrance, Sr. with toddler Terrance, Jr.

Last photo of Terrance, Sr. and Terrance, Jr. with Mom, taken by Sherri.

Chapter 28

HOW INFORMATION BECOMES TRANSFORMATION

Nephew finished his first level of nursing training and passed his California boards to become licensed as a Certified Nursing Assistant. He immediately received numerous job offers in California and New Mexico. He decided to stay in California to be closer to his children and to finish his training to become an ordained minister in his new church.

He first started studying to become a minister long before considering nursing. I remembered sending him tuition for his first set of professional religious education classes. Four years ago, his ministerial quest had been derailed when he had a child with another woman in his former church. Indeed, the woman felt so embarrassed that Nephew was the father of her child that she initially didn't tell anyone, including Nephew. When she finally revealed the truth, that meant three of Nephew's children were accompanied by their mothers to Sunday service at the same church. His father, Terrance, Sr., was the first to show me a picture of Nephew's fourth child who looked just like him.

Terrance dubbed the mothers as Nephew's "Church Harem." They were all model tall. The minister booted Nephew from his ministerial training school for lack of discernment and good judgment.

After several years of trying to make amends, Nephew accepted that the minister would never relent and permit him to become licensed at his house of worship. He switched churches.

My grandfather (Nephew's great-grandfather) also experienced a tumultuous path to the ministry. Aunt Liz and Uncle John told me that he had initially resisted his call to ministry and had spontaneously gone blind. It was only after he accepted the call to become ordained that his eyesight was miraculously restored. While lecturing at one religious convocation, Grandpa stood before a hushed audience with outstretched hands. He encouraged the congregation to:

> Burn up "oh don't"
>
> Throw away "oh if"
>
> Send "oh can't" to the county farm
>
> Because it CAN BE DONE

The phrases seared themselves into the memories of Uncle John and Aunt Liz, who repeated them to me often in rhythmic cadence to remind me to accept challenges that came my way, just as Grandpa had done.

Grandpa's father, Mance Easter, had experienced different challenges as a minister. Ku Klux Klan members showed up to his home after they began reorganizing in Arkansas after 1915. One afternoon, Mance, who had been born in 1863 (according to his tombstone) in Magnolia during the height of the Civil War, heard a ruckus outside of his home and stepped out onto his porch.

A Ku Klux Klan leader demanded, "Send the boy out."

Mance, according to Uncle John and Aunt Liz, stared at the Klansmen gathered below him. They were all wearing white robes that partially shielded their faces. A Black man with skin the color of pasteurized butter, Mance stood erect at six-feet, five-inches tall. With his hands at his side, he calmly told the Klansmen, "I won't send the boy out, but you can come in and get him."

The Klan members briefly conferred among themselves. They left and never returned.

Upon hearing Uncle John and Aunt Liz recount this tale of family history, I marveled at Mance's courage to stand up to the draped menace. Klansmen hid inside robes meant to intimidate, yet Mance Easter refused to be bullied into giving up one of his sons to a violent fate, such as decades later befell Emmett Till after a white woman falsely accused him of flirting with her.

Growing up in Phoenix, Granny often recounted how men connected to the Klan kidnapped Emmett Till from his grandparents' Mississippi Delta home and then tortured and mutilated his fourteen-year-old body. His mother, Mamie, ordered an open casket at her son's public funeral in Chicago so the world could see what the Klan had done to her boy. An all-white jury acquitted Emmett Till's murderers, although the two men admitted to the killing in a 1956 interview with Look Magazine. Till's accuser, Carolyn Bryant Donham, admitted she lied on the witness stand about him to an interviewer in 2008. She died in 2023.

Mance Easter did not give the Klan a chance to butcher his son. By telling the Klansmen they could come in and "get the boy," Mance challenged their commitment. Were they willing to step inside a man's home to obtain his son? To do so would be to put their own lives in jeopardy because they had no idea what weapons Mance Easter had and who was inside with "the boy" holding those weapons.

By going into the ministry, Nephew was following trails that had been laid down by his ancestors. Uncle John, himself, had become a minister late in his life. His challenge was different because, following his return from serving in the Vietnam War, he had developed a penchant for peppering his talk with four letter words. I asked Aunt Liz, who attended his church, whether Uncle John was able to get through a sermon without using them. "Occasionally," she said, "one will escape." Fortunately, none escaped during the time he preached and performed master of ceremony duties at his sister Ida's funeral services. Nephew was unable to attend, but I read Langston Hughes' poem, "Dreams."

Dreams

Hold fast to dreams
For if dreams die
Life is a broken-winged bid
That cannot fly.

Hold fast to dreams
For when dreams go
Life is a barren field
Frozen with snow.

Since Aunt Ida had been a teacher, I felt it appropriate to share one of my favorite poems and one that I knew she would like. It puts forth eternal good advice.

When Uncle John died in 2023, I put together his funeral program and brought in Nephew, as a minister in training, to lead the congregants through prayers and through the "Ashes to Ashes, Dust to Dust" ritual as Uncle John's casket was lowered into the ground. All the events were held at the Veterans chapel and cemetery south of Las Vegas. A second cousin hosted repast and then Nephew piled three of his children into the backseat and drove back to California.

On Sunday, October 26, 2025, Nephew, dressed up in a new suit and polished black shoes, greeted me at his new church home. I had flown in from Albuquerque the day before to take his family out to dinner. At the seafood restaurant overlooking Redondo Beach, I met his fifth and final child, along with her mother. Following the child's birth and our subsequent conversation on my front porch when we were caring for Mom, Nephew elected to have a vasectomy.

As I sat in the front row, beaming with pride, the minister called the service to order with prayers and songs. He then introduced me. I held up a Bible and explained that it had first been gifted to Nephew by my mother/his grandmother when he was ten years of age. She had signed it over to her grandson from herself, me, and his uncle Ralph, and saved this Bible among her collection. The initial timing for the Bible's purchase had coincided with our family trip to Hope, Arkansas, when Nephew had just finished fifth grade. Nephew teared up as I explained the Bible's history. It felt as if Mom and Ralph's spirits were in the church with us.

Holding the family Bible, Nephew preached. He discussed "how information can become transformation" if people are willing to process the material and learn. He used his struggles with alcohol addiction and weight gain as an example. "I can write anyone a plan for losing weight, but to look at me you wouldn't believe I followed it," he said to chuckles from the audience.

He added, "I had a toxic relationship with alcohol. I was best friends with alcohol." By letting alcohol go, he said that he had gone through a process of sanctification and was now transformed. He had taken his last drink on March 14, 2023, over two years before.

"We have a way that we want our life to look," Nephew continued, "but you must process the information for it to lead to transformation in your life. Strive for your life to reflect what you believe."

I sat in the front seat, enraptured by his energetic presentation. I listened, thinking about all the pathways I had encouraged him to avoid by using contracts. Nevertheless, he had followed the trails leading to alcohol, overeating, and abundance of females anyway. It took a willingness to stop drinking to change his life. Only he could make the decision to cease overeating and having children.

After Nephew finished his sermon, all the ministers in the church prayed over him while he knelt in front of the podium. The lead minister presented his license. With the stroke of a pen, Nephew became a fifth-generation American man of the cloth in our family.

On that family trip to Hope with Mom and Ralph when Nephew was ten, the year Mom purchased his Bible, we had visited Mance Easter's graveside and said prayers for his soul. A quarter of a century later, Nephew had now found his future in the paths laid down by his ancestors.

Rev. S.P. Easter and his license

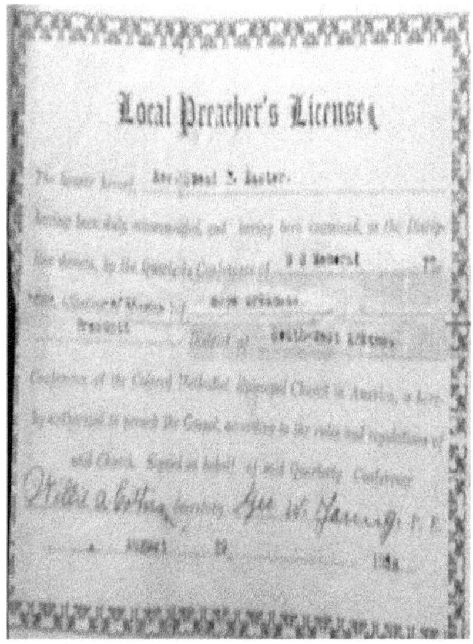

Local Preacher's License

Rev. and Mrs. Easter (Grampa and Granny) at Trinity Temple CME Church in Tucson, AZ

Nephew with his ministerial license

Nephew preaching.

Chapter 29

HERE'S THE PHONE

Many friends and acquaintances initially expressed pity when I told them my 12-year-old nephew was moving in with me to attend seventh grade in Albuquerque. "Poor you" or "You're in for a big surprise" were the two comments I heard the most often. A year later after my friends met Nephew and witnessed my smooth-running household, the comments became, "How did you do it?" or "I wish I had gotten my son to do more work around the house when he was growing up."

I deployed what I termed a lawyer's approach to parenting by contracts. The agreement that worked best was the division of chores accompanied by the payment of an allowance. My house ran more smoothly and stayed cleaner. Nephew learned financial responsibility because he only got paid his full allowance for finishing his chores. This tracks real life. Most people find that if they don't show up for the full hours of their job, they get paid less than their full wages or lose their jobs. Then they don't have enough money to pay bills or to spend on their personal needs. I only had to deduct from Nephew's allowance once for him to understand this truism. He saved money to go to the movies and buy what he wanted, including the bicycle that he purchased and never lost his privileges to ride.

At a conference at the George Washington Law School in the fall of 2004, I recounted the story of publishing what eventually became three academic books in a year, mentioning as a sidenote that I was fortunate to have my nephew living with me. For instance, if I realized that I was not going to get home until exactly 6:00 p.m., I called at 5:30 p.m. to ask my nephew to prepare dinner.

That evening at the reception, law professor Emma Coleman Jordan came up to me and started bowing. She said, "Writing three books in a year is impressive, but you deserve a genius award for getting at 14-year-old to cook and clean. My 14-year-old daughter was hiding from me when I returned home today because she hadn't cleaned the kitchen. She waited till her older sister came home before she would reveal herself."

I thanked Professor Jordan for her compliments. My belief is that it is never too late or too early to start training kids in essential life skills. They need to learn to take care of themselves during childhood and adolescence. As adults, they will be expected to feed themselves and keep their surroundings livable. They will also be expected to hold down jobs, to show up for work on time, and to manage their finances. Where are they going to learn to be adults if not from their parents or parental figures?

During the years Nephew lived with me, sometimes I received snide comments about his work around the house like, "This is child abuse." In my opinion, it's child abuse *not* to give children life skills.

Of course, not all my ideas worked as intended. For example – The Basketball Contract. As much as I was trying to create incentives to keep Nephew focused on his grades, this contract was far too stringent.

Contract between Nephew and Auntie
Re: Basketball

Nephew acknowledges the following:

Basketball is a privilege not a right.

Privileges flow from doing his homework, chores, and generally contributing to family life.

He will strive to be a scholar-athlete and not an athletic student, meaning he will put his schoolwork before basketball or other sports.

I. Nephew agrees to the following:

a. On his next report card, he must produce a minimum of a 2.8 average to remain on the Jefferson basketball team.

b. On the progress report that follows his next report card, his grades must rise to a minimum of 3.0 to remain on the team.

c. On his second report card, his grades must rise to a minimum of 3.2 to remain on the team.

II. If Nephew does not meet the above minimum grade point averages, he will resign from the team or Auntie will notify the coach that he is no longer available.

This contract is dated Thursday, October 17, 2002, and signed by:

____________________ ____________________

Nephew Auntie

If I had to do it all over again, I would have sat the GPA numbers lower, like 2.3 or 2.5. It was after I made this mistake (see chapters 9-10) that I realized joining the team was meaningful for Nephew and it kept him engaged with life.

Some affluent parents think they should just give their offspring money because they can afford it. This approach misses the point. Allowances are about kids learning self-responsibility and not about the ability of parents to be generous. Some parents gift money and presents as a substitute for spending time with their children. If you took a poll of most kids, you would probably find that they are more likely to associate love with time spent with their parents or parental figures than with the money spent on them.

Another lesson that flowed from my experiences was the importance of the family dinners together about six nights a week Additionally, we often dined together for Saturday breakfast and Sunday brunch. It was during these meals that he kept me informed about his life. While I didn't always want to hear the details about what he was doing with girls or his description of one or two as having "a nice juicy butt," I did listen to him. Sometimes, I fought the temptation to put my hands over my ears as I felt he was sharing too much information. However, for someone who is a parent or who suddenly becomes a parent of a preteen or teen, you can never hear too much. For parents and parental figures, listening to their children is part of the job description.

My approach was borne out by a study that proved teenagers who had dinner with their families at least five nights a week were less likely to become sexually active or to indulge in drugs. Even though teens seek independence and like to pretend that parents are irrelevant, they still need parents to set boundaries, to indicate the lines between behavior that is right and is wrong. They do not want to be set adrift in the world. They want to know that someone is in charge, that someone cares.

Toward the end of seventh grade, Nephew surprised me by coming home with bad grades and immediately saying, "Here's the phone." That he voluntarily gave up his phone privileges caught me by surprise. Another time he did something inappropriate, he asked, "So, what's the punishment?"

He came to expect that there would be consequences for bad behavior and that he wouldn't be allowed to get away with anything. He also seemed happier when consequences were imposed. It was if he was glad that someone was monitoring his life and was on top of it.

While I was proud that Nephew did not become sexually active as he was going through puberty under my watch, I was sad when he crossed this boundary in high school. Once he confessed to me, I begged him to tell his mother, but he refused. Since I had given my word not to divulge the information to her, I did not. This was hard for me because I felt she should know, but I also wanted to keep open communication so he continued to share information with me, no matter how painful the situation might be.

Eventually, Nephew's mother found a condom in his room in Long Beach. Once she imposed a month's physical separation between him and the girl, he seemed much happier. When I talked to him before she knew he had become sexually active, he seemed weighted down by the secret and lies. I just happened to call the day she found out and had imposed punishment. There was more joy in his voice that day than I had heard in the several months since his return to California.

I also thought it important to share information with Nephew's teachers. At Jefferson Middle School's open house at the beginning of the year, I left my business card with my home phone number and email address on the back with each teacher. I asked each one to please contact me if he or she experienced any trouble with my nephew. If I received an email or call from a teacher, Nephew heard about it. I supported all of his teachers because I felt they had his best interest at heart.

Some parents argue with teachers about their kids' grades instead of asking what can be done to help the kid improve. The first communication will be received by the teacher as an attack; the second will be received warmly as genuine interest in helping the kid develop skills and talents.

As a university professor, I have had parents intervene on behalf of law students. Although this represents the 17th to 19th years of education for students who began with kindergarten, some parents can't seem to help themselves. One law school parent emailed me, seeking a higher grade for her son while making excuses for his failure to take an assignment seriously. Another mother emailed me requesting that her daughter be given special dispensation to complete an assignment either earlier or later so that she could fly back to the east coast to be fitted for her wedding gown. I wondered if these helicopter mothers planned to call judges to obtain extensions to file briefs or urge law firms to excuse their children's tardiness at work.

Much to his credit, when Nephew received a "D" grade on his final eighth-grade report card, he took full responsibility. I asked him if he wanted to appeal the grade since I had heard other teachers complain about the teacher who gave him the "D" grade. Indeed, Nephew had told stories about how the teacher ate food in class, spent time playing on the computer, harassed girls, and didn't teach his students anything. When he first started receiving lower grades on his progress report, I encouraged him to ignore how he felt about the teacher and do the work anyway. However, he couldn't do it and let the teacher get inside his head. In the end, he said, "I earned that grade, Auntie. I didn't like him, and I didn't do the work."

There was nothing more to be said. Hooray to Nephew for taking responsibility for his choices and their consequences.

Overall, my experience parenting Nephew was joyful. I started writing this book because I missed hearing his laughter in the halls, smelling the aroma of his cooking in the kitchen, and feeling the cleanliness of the car that he handwashed weekly during his stay. For every minute of frustration, there were probably five minutes or more when I burst into laughter at something he said or did. We all know that laughter is good for the soul and healthy for the body. Kids who feel secure by the boundaries that parents provide can be a pleasure to have around. Parents owe it to themselves and to their kids to provide that safety net.

Happy parenting!

ACKNOWLEDGEMENTS

I write to thank the many individuals who have read chapters or the entire manuscript of this book. After Nephew read the entire manuscript, he told me how much he loved the book and that he wanted to include information about the abuse he suffered as a child. He thought this might give readers a better understanding of the dynamics of what happened when he moved in with me as a twelve-year-old. Nephew also thought it important to let the readers know that his grandfather had been left by his first wife which may explain why he kidnapped the three children he had with my mother. These additions were painful to write.

The members of my various critique groups provided important feedback over the years, including Judith Avila, Sue Brown, Melody Groves, Kathleen Hessler, Phil Jackson, Jon Miller, Sue Mann, Patty Allred, Donna Pedace, Joann Hamlin, Carolyn Wheelock, Susan Wyatt, Kay Lamb, Kathy Kitts, Carol Kreis, Ella Joan Fenoglio and Jeane McKenna. I thank law student Annie Counter for conducting a beta read of the manuscript.

I express gratitude to Rose Marie Kern for her interior design of this book. Rosa Amijo-Pemble, with *Images by Rosa*, designed the cover by incorporating

Rosa's images of a pumpkin patch and the Sandia Mountains in Albuquerque, NM, to creatively showcase a photo that I shot of my nephew at age 7, text I provided, and a photo taken by Denise Tessier, on one of our hikes in the Sandia Mountains in Albuquerque.

OTHER BOOKS BY SHERRI BURR

A Short & Happy Guide to Financial Well-being (West Academic, 2014, 2nd Ed., 2021) (won First Place in the New Mexico-Arizona Book Awards for best Business Books)

Art Law: Cases and Materials (with DuBoff and Murray) (William S. Hein & Co., 2004)

Art Law: Cases & Materials (Revised Edition) (with DuBoff and Murray) (Aspen, 2010)

Art Law: Cases & Materials' Teachers' Manual (with DuBoff and Murray) (Aspen, 2010)

*Complicated Lives: Free Blacks in Virginia, **1619-1865*** (Carolina Academic Press, 2019) (Nominated for the Pulitzer Prize in History)

Entertainment Law: Cases and Materials in Existing and Emerging Media (West Academic, 2011, 2nd Ed., 2017, 3rd Ed., 2021, 4th Ed., 2024)

Entertainment Law: Cases and Materials in Existing and Emerging Media's Teachers Manual (West, 2011, 2nd Ed., 2017, 3rd Ed., 2021, 4th Ed., 2024)

Entertainment Law: Cases and Materials in Film, Television, and Music (with Henslee) (ThomsonWest 2004)

Entertainment Law in a Nutshell (ThomsonWest 2004); 2nd Ed., 2007, 3rd Ed., 2012, 4th Ed., 2017, Chinese translation published in 2018, 5th Ed., 2022, 6th Ed., 2024)

Modern Intellectual Property and Unfair Competition Law (with Kitch & Perlman) (Foundation Press, 6th Ed., 2014)

Modern Intellectual Property and Unfair Competition Law Teacher's Manual (with Kitch & Perlman) (West 2014)

Quick Review of International law (West, 2006; 2nd Ed., 2008, 3rd Ed., 2015, 4th Ed., 2020)

Sum & Substance on International Law Audio book (ThomsonWest 2006, 2nd Ed., 2013, 3rd Ed., 2020, 4th Ed., 2025)

Wills & Trusts in a Nutshell 3rd Ed. (with Mennell) (ThomsonWest 2007, 4th Ed., 2013 5th Ed., 2017, 6th Ed., 2022)

Sum & Substance on Entertainment Law Audio Book (West, 2008) (2nd Ed., 2019, 3rd Ed., 2025)

ABOUT THE AUTHOR

Photo by Denise Tessier

SHERRI BURR lives in Albuquerque, NM, where she has won numerous awards as an author, lecturer, and television producer.

In 2025, she received the Parris Award from Southwest Writers, the organization's highest honor for a published writer who has contributed substantially to the organization and to advance other writers.

In 2024, she was selected as the inaugural Black Women United for Action Fellow at the George Washington Presidential Library. Mount Holyoke College presented her its Alumni Achievement Award in 2022. In 2021, the National Federation of Press Women announced her as the winner of its highest award, Communicator of Achievement. Also, in 2021, the National Council of Negro Women Albuquerque Section presented her its Dr. Mary McLeod Bethune Legacy Award for "outstanding Achievements in Literacy and Leadership Support for the Community."

Burr has also produced and hosted television talk shows *ARTS TALK* and *Dating 101.* Burr's hobbies include cooking, hiking, golfing, with occasional doses of horseback riding and kayaking.

The poem on the next page by Nephew, Terrance Peete Jr., was published in *You're Seeing It Through My Eyes*, two years after he participated in the inaugural O'Keeffe Leadership Program for Boys. The title of the booklet was taken from the last line of Nephew's poem.

Alex Freeman and Nick Pumilia, Eds., *You're Seeing It Through My Eyes: A Collection of Work Written by the Participants of the O'Keeffe Art and Leadership Program for Boys*, Page 7 (Santa Fe, NM: George O'Keeffe Museum, Summer, 2004)

Living with Nephew

Clear air to breathe
As I sit with bent knees
Cloudy skies big and black
Ready to let rain go down my back
Green trees growing and dying
As the birds go overhead soaring and flying

Life is good when I'm in the neighborhood
But life is great when the world awaits
Awaits to come
Back to reality
But this is reality in a different state

Living my life
And it's wonderful and great
As I watch things grow
In the open range

I love where I am
And this is where I want to be
With the sky overhead
And I can stretch and breathe
Living under the open sky

This could be your life
But right now its mine
And you're seeing it through my eyes

Terrance Peete Jr., Age 12 at the time of writing

www.ingramcontent.com/pod-product-compliance
Ingram Content Group UK Ltd.
Pitfield, Milton Keynes, MK11 3LW, UK
UKHW060116010826
14089UKWH00003B/8

9 798990 424982